Sharon Fern...

111 Places
in New Delhi
That You Must
Not Miss

Photographs by Tarunima Sen

emons:

Did you enjoy it? Do you want more?
Join us in uncovering new places around the world on:
www.111places.com

Foreword

Delhi, "the city of cities," is also a city of storytellers. Its blue signboards, sandstone monuments, and even its trees have enthralling tales to share — tales of the past and the present. From Ibn Batuta and Khushwant Singh to Amir Khusro and William Dalrymple, the shadows of literary giants loom large for anyone attempting to write about Delhi. Yet it is these very shadows that guide you through this city that has been shaped by grand sultanates and ambitious colonialists.

Each neighbourhood — old and new — bears a unique personality that leaves a life-long impression on the beholder. The winding lanes of old Chandni Chowk transform into a maze in vacation scrapbooks. The creaky rhythm of cycle-rickshaw pedals becomes a soundtrack for your travel stories. The sprawling gardens and avenues of Luytens' Delhi evolve into nostalgic bookmarks.

Delhi, as an experience, is greater than the sum of its parts. For me, Delhi represents India, in all its unwieldiness, its contradictions, and its diversity. I have tried to capture this mixed bag of feelings that Delhi evokes with the 111 colourful and esoteric places included in these pages. There is the Delhi of Sufis, the Delhi of Emperors, the "modern" Delhi, and of course, the "foodie" Delhi. This collection of little-known places forms the ethos of a sprawling city filled with undiscovered locales, crumbling edifices, and a culture to which the cliché "melting pot" truly applies.

The moment I thought I had unravelled a bit of Delhi, it led me further into a world where princesses wrote poems, Sufis performed miracles, poets lay forgotten in their graves, and tombs were reborn as traffic circles. This is my Delhi. And now it is yours too.

111 Places

1_ A Godin & Co.

Official piano tuners to Lord Mountbatten

The gleaming white baby-grand piano, enjoying pride of place in the centre of this shop, draws in casual strollers even if they have no intention of buying an instrument. The knowledgeable staff members at A Godin & Co., accustomed to gawkers, are indulgent, and humour curious walk-ins. There's an air of aloofness among the huddle of the shiny black pianos that have a dedicated section at the back of the shop. It is as if they know that they lounge in a hallowed musical space. Even the street gets quieter as one nears this landmark. For this is no ordinary music store. Its legacy goes back to 1900 in Quetta, Pakistan.

As with most of the oldest business concerns in Delhi, the Partition of 1947 was a turning point for A Godin. After Independence, the shop saw a rise in the popularity of classical Indian instruments among its patrons. So, while the haughty pianos maintain their distance, the front of the store features sitars and tablas, sharing a harmonious space with violins and saxophones. The refurbished, modern-looking shop receives a lot of interest in pianos nowadays, however, probably more than the days when English civil servants rented pianos for a monthly fee.

A Godin & Co. has been housed in the Regal Building since the 1950s. A certificate proclaiming the store as the tuners to Lord Mountbatten is hung hidden from view on a wall in the inner section. There is no attempt to highlight this illustrious customer. Celiano Godin, founder of the store, has had musical greats like Elton John, Ravi Shankar, and Brian Silas walk in through these doors over the years.

As a young budding musician stops in and heads for a piano, notes of popular artist Sam Smith's *Stay With Me* fill the room. These are far removed from the classical strains heard in the store during the days of the Raj; but though the notes may have changed, the music plays on at A Godin & Co.

Address 1, Regal Building, Parliament Street, Tel +91 11 23362809 | **Getting there** Patel Chowk Metro Station (Yellow Line) | **Hours** Mon–Sat 11am–7pm | **Tip** Watch a matinée at the Regal, one of Delhi's oldest cinema houses. With sepia photographs of film stars lining the walls, and a grand staircase that leads to the balcony seating, the Regal's atmosphere is a throwback to the black-and-white movie era.

2 _ Abdur Rahim Khan-i-Khana's Tomb

The plundered tomb that still shines

Better known as Khankhana by locals, the tomb that stands in plain sight is among the most overlooked monuments in Delhi. Few know the story of Abdur Rahim, fewer still of his tomb's existence in the shadow of the grand Humayun's Tomb complex, nearby.

This gentle giant of a monument, with vestiges of water channels and pools, stands proud on a square platform covering arched cells. The sandstone structure, once a glorious landmark, was stripped of its marble slabs and other ornamentals, which were used to build Safdarjung's tomb. Delicate floral and geometrical carvings and the remnants of a magnificent peacock struggle to survive among its defaced walls.

The story of Abdur Rahim Khan-i-Khana (1556–1627) has been lost to time. A respected general commanding a huge army in the court of Akbar, Abdur Rahim is remembered more for his poetry than his military career. His keen interest in astrology and linguistics, as well as his understanding of warfare, led Akbar to entrust his son Jahangir's tutelage to him. In a twist of fate, Abdur Rahim's two sons were killed by Jahangir when they opposed his ascension to the throne of Delhi. Bereft of family, wealth, and power towards the end of his days, Abdur Rahim died a broken man.

Though little is known of the man who wrote them, his *dohas* (Hindi couplets) live on. One of his popular *dohas* reflects upon the wisdom and heart of a great man: "When I set out to look for evil, I found no one wicked. When I searched my own heart, I found there was none as evil as I."

Once an inspiration for the Taj Mahal, Khan-i-Khana's tomb is a peaceful oasis adjacent to a busy thoroughfare. As motor vehicles zip by, it still offers a poetic vista – a reminder of the time when poet Tulsidas and Abdur Rahim spoke to each other in couplets.

Address Mathura Road, Nizamuddin West | **Getting there** JLN Stadium Metro Station (Violet Line) | **Hours** Daily, sunrise to sunset. Admission fee: Rs 100 for foreign tourists. | **Tip** Tee off at the Delhi Golf Club (Dr Zakir Hussain Marg, Lodhi Colony) with peacocks that monitor your swing. Not a golfer? Then sip a martini or a cup of tea, or discover the hidden monuments on the courses. You will need a member to accompany you.

3__Ahinsa Sthal
A place of peaceful existence

This tiny, well-manicured, and lush park calls out to the world-weary to come soothe their souls for a while. At the centre of the park a 14-foot-tall Lord Mahavira statue, installed by Jain worshippers in the mid-1980s, affords a panoramic view from its pedestal. Stray visitors mostly chance upon the statue while visiting the Qutb Minar.

Few are aware of the historic significance of the statue of the last *tirthankar* (pure soul) of Jainism. The first battle of Tarain (1192) was a significant battle in Delhi's history. It was the first time Muhammad Ghauri attacked what was then the territory of Rajput king Prithviraj Chauhan. Ghauri was defeated, but when he returned with a larger army a year later, he prevailed and executed the Rajput king. After vanquishing several kingdoms and rulers, he returned to Afghanistan, leaving his slave-commander Muhammed Aibak in charge. Aibak, a devout Muslim, destroyed several temples in the Mehrauli area. It is believed that they were stripped to construct the Quwwat-ul-Islam, the country's earliest mosque. As Mughal power diminished, people demanded that the mosque be felled. But the Jains, adhering to their tenets of non-violence, built the Ahinsa Sthal. Seated in Padmasana pose on a lotus flower, Mahavira overlooks Mehrauli, with its profusion of structures belonging to different religions.

Incidentally, this was the site where British resident Thomas Metcalfe's summer home, Battery House, stood. His idea of a house by the ocean was definitely a misplaced notion in a landlocked city, with Metcalfe's Folly (see p. 142) visible in the distance. Now, stone *apsaras* (celestial maidens) mischievously peep out of the thick foliage, musicians play silent tunes, and poems pepper the walls with wisdom. One line reads, "I shall not be too proud nor shall I be angry towards anyone." Behind the Mahavira statue, the colour of the sky is a glorious gold, stained by the setting sun.

Address Mehrauli Bypass, Mehrauli | Getting there Saket Metro Station (Yellow Line) |
Hours Tue–Sun 11am–9pm | Tip Qila Rai Pithora (Qila Rai Pithora, Sainik Farm),
which also incorporates the Lal Kot, is a 12th-century fort from where the Tomar Rajputs,
Prithviraj Chauhan, and the slave dynasties ruled Delhi. The bastions and gateways still
remain and a statue of Prithviraj Chauhan in the Qila Rai complex is a reminder of the
first city of Delhi.

4_Ashokan Rock Edict
Delhi's original edict

This is the story of a bloody war that changed the course of history. The carnage of the infamous Battle of Kalinga (261 BC) left more than 100,000 dead on the battlefield and forcibly evicted 150,000 others. As a victor surveying his winnings, Emperor Ashoka, one of history's greatest conquerors, saw monks trying to bring solace to the dying. It was an experience that transformed him; he gave up his imperialist ambitions and embraced Buddhism.

Ashoka's adoption of the Buddhist religion brought peace to his kingdom, which stretched across the Indian subcontinent. Desirous of sharing his newfound spiritual and religious wisdom with his populace, he inscribed his learning, teachings, and messages on rocks. These 36 edicts, written in Prakrit using the Brahmi script, were installed throughout India. Of these, three are now in Delhi. Two of these are pillar edicts, and were transported from the cities of Meerut and Ambala by Feroz Shah Tughluq. One of them can be seen outside Hindu Rao Hospital, and the other is at Ferozshah Kotla Fort.

The only edict original to Delhi is located close to the Kalkaji Temple, in South Delhi. Discovered in 1966 by a building contractor, it was examined by archaeologists and found to be similar to 13 other rock edicts. This one is considered the 14th engraving. Sitting on a grassy hillock, protected by an unsightly concrete and metal cage, the rock inscriptions are faint. The only visitors are Buddhists from around the world, who tie prayer flags to the cage (which is sometimes opened for a curious individual). Children fly kites at this pit stop on the ancient trade route. It is also said that the rock was installed at the site of an old temple.

His message of striving for *dhamma* (the right path) is clear in intent and perhaps lives on in spirit in an urban colony that has the ISKCON temple, Kalkaji temple, and Buddha Vihar, all nearby.

Address Srinivaspuri, near the ISKCON temple, Raja Dhir Sain Marg | **Getting there** Kalkaji Mandir Metro Station (Violet Line) | **Hours** Daily, sunrise to sunset | **Tip** The Lotus Temple (Lotus Temple Rd, Shambhu Dayal Bagh, Bahapur), a lotus-shaped architectural marvel propagating the Baha'i faith, is close to the edict.

5__Atgah Khan's Tomb

A token of an emperor's love

Lost in the urban sprawl of Nizamuddin, the tomb of Emperor Akbar's foster father, Atgah Khan, is a respectful token of love built in 1566–67. The white marble and deep red sandstone weave a tale of political aspiration and crude jealousy into the tombs of Atgah Khan and Adham Khan. In death they remain bonded by the hatred that led to their ends.

A farmer's son, Shamsuddin Muhammad started out as a soldier and rose through the ranks. His wife Jiji Angah was chosen as one of Akbar's wet nurses. He helped Emperor Humayun escape Sher Shah Suri and was a trusted court member. In recognition of his service, Humayun bestowed upon him the title *Atgah*, meaning "foster father"; and after Humayun's death, Atgah Khan became the orphaned boy-emperor Akbar's advisor in administrative, army, and personal matters. When Atgah Khan was appointed *wakil* (prime minister), a jealous Adham Khan (son of another wet nurse) murdered him in the Diwan-i-Khas. Akbar, in turn, had Adham Khan thrown from a terrace, not once but twice, as punishment – a doubly tortuous death indeed.

Under Akbar's instructions, Mirza Aziz Kotah, Atgah Khan's son, undertook the construction of his father's tomb. In every tiled wall and latticed stone of the tomb, there is a tribute to the man who stood by the side of the boy-emperor. The tomb showcases a combination of different Mughal styles, such as *pietra dura* work, calligraphy, and medallions.

Like many Mughal monuments, Atgah Khan's tomb served as a refuge to the displaced during the Partition. Surrounded by brick houses, the tomb, located in a courtyard with a small metal gate, remains hidden from sight. The wooden door to the tomb is locked to prevent it from misuse. A pavilion and a once-beautiful *mihrab* (wall that indicates the direction of Mecca), with delicate tile work, serve as a backyard to the families living in the complex.

Address Near Hazrat Nizamuddin Dargah, Nizamuddin Basti | Getting there Jangpura
Metro Station (Violet Line) or Pragati Maidan Metro Station (Blue Line) | Hours Daily,
sunrise to sunset | Tip Ghalib's, a famous restaurant in the lanes of Nizamuddin, is known
for its melt-in-your-mouth kebabs.

6__ The Attic

A secret cultural club

On a quiet section of Parliament Street, flanked by a clothing store and a dry cleaner and two flights up a wooden staircase, is the Attic. It was once a personal museum of sorts, host to private exhibits of inherited heirlooms, textiles, art, and jewellery. It spun off from these beginnings into an organic performance and gallery space that throws up surprises every so often. Even though it is right in the heart of Delhi's first colonial-era shopping mall, Connaught Place, it remains a little-known secret of the city.

What the Attic lacks in size, it makes up for in heart. Divided into three sections, the 1,000-square-foot wood-panelled space is warm and welcoming, with a relaxed vibe. A large window in the cloakroom-*cum*-reception-area frames the tiny vestibule, which features bookshelves, a few stacked chairs, and a casual mountain of floor cushions. A versatile, well-lit larger gallery with stark white walls follows. Cleverly, this also works as a space to seat an audience. Further ahead is "the stage," with mud walls; separated from the main room by only a curtain, it is an intimate theatrical setting for both the audience and the talent.

"Expect the unexpected" certainly applies here. The Attic showcases an eclectic range of talent and topics. One day there could be a mindful eating workshop, another day a solo theatre performance, a music recital, a themed poetry reading, a film screening, a photography exhibit, an Italian cooking class, or an alternative telling of *Alice in Wonderland* in Urdu. During one visit, an artist was rehearsing for an upcoming event at a small pulpit, which brought to mind a certain Shakespearean drama involving a balcony. A democratic venue, it hosts young artists, old poets, classical dancers, filmmakers, environmentalists, and open-mic amateurs. It's a unique creative "space for the living arts" where the spectators and performers are all part of the drama.

Address 36 Regal Building, Parliament Street, Connaught Place, www.theatticdelhi.org, info@theatticdelhi.com | **Getting there** Rajiv Chowk Metro Station (Blue & Yellow Lines) | **Hours** Event based | **Tip** The Shop (10 Regal Building), just down the road, is a delightful boutique that offers handcrafted textiles and products that are ethnically influenced but contemporary in style.

7 __ Azadpur Mandi
Asia's largest wholesale vegetable market

Nowhere is the change of seasons more evident than at the Azadpur Mandi, located just off the Grand Trunk Road. Seasonal vegetables and fruits weighing thousands of kilograms find their way to the Azadpur Subzi Mandi (vegetable market) that's been here since 1977. The place is filled with colour, sounds, and scents – sometimes pleasant and sometimes plain rotten. Porters lug nylon, net, and jute sacks of potatoes, cabbage, cauliflower, peas, pumpkins, oranges, apples, watermelons, and other produce that you might never have seen before. Traders are happy to jump in and tell you more about how the special pumpkins come in from West Bengal, and at times even share a basic recipe to get you started.

This is not one of those markets that have an intense burst of activity in the early hours and then fall into a drowsy lull for the rest of the day. Truckloads of produce arrive morning, noon, and night; the bidding and dealing of auctions are constant in this market that never sleeps. There's even a timetable for when *kacchi sabziya* (raw vegetables), fruits, and hardier vegetables like potatoes and onions arrive.

In the chaos and arcane appearance of the *mandi*, billions of rupees exchange hands. Even the deals follow old methods of hidden handshakes and under-the-kerchief pacts – although these take time to spot, since technology is changing customs.

Around 15,000 tonnes of exotic, local, and rare produce pass through the nondescript, makeshift stalls of the massive *mandi*, spread over 75 acres. Every corner offers delightful sights: a load of lemons is weighed in one stall, crates of peaches are delivered to another, and an assortment of green herbs is arranged in baskets elsewhere. The vibrant market revels in its connection with the farmers and the land, a refreshing experience for city slickers who are used to Saran-wrapped, sterile produce picked from supermarket shelves.

Address Adarsh Nagar New Sabji Mandi, Azadpur | Getting there Adarsh Nagar Metro Station (Yellow Line) | Hours All day | Tip On the walls of the Delhi Cold Storage building next to the Azadpur Mosque, Axel Void's riveting graffiti, which is part of a series called *Mediocre*, stops people in their tracks. A dark wall with a single candle burning beside a fruit platter and a knife with the Hindi word *Zindagi* ("Life") inscribed on it is fitting for the market that provides sustenance to this city of cities.

8___Babu Shahi Bawarchi

A dinner fit for emperors

In Delhi, *biryani* is more than just seasoned rice with meat or vegetables. It is an obsession. Everyone has a personal favourite, and the choice of ingredients, duration of cooking, material of the vessel, type of fire, and even the use of a ladle (or not) become bones of contention. Seemingly pleasant people are immediately divided into conflicting factions. If there is one *biryani* that brings a ceasefire to many a well-informed table, it is Babu Shahi Bawarchi's *biryani*.

This consensus-generating delicacy comes from a small, open-air restaurant with deep cultural roots. There couldn't be a more surreal spot for a meal. Set in the courtyard of the Hazrat Matka Shah Baba shrine, the eatery is surrounded by trees. The branches of these trees – which reach for the sky, where the divine meets earthly desires and wishes – are bedecked with earthen pots, offerings of gratitude made by believers at the shrine, in exchange for wishes granted. The call of the muezzin creates an ideal atmosphere for the stories that swirl along with the fragrance of rose petals, incense, and the perfect bowl of *biryani*.

Annu *bhai* (a masculine endearment), the owner of this small eatery, can trace his lineage to the head chef in the kitchens of Emperor Shahjahan. The stories of emperors rewarding their courtiers with *biryani* from this family's kitchen aren't volunteered as easily by Annu *bhai* as they used to be by his father, the late Babu Khan. The rudimentary setting of bare benches, a metal table, and the presence of the shrine above may deter a lot of Delhiites from dining here. However, they show their love for the place by ordering kilos of this limited menu over the phone.

Only true gourmands and pilgrims venture to this nondescript eatery. Perhaps that is the reason why it remains a secret of the "inner circle" of Delhi.

Address Shop No 5, Dargah Matka Peer, Mathura Road, Pragati Maidan, opposite NSI Club, Tel +91 11 23371454 | **Getting there** Pragati Maidan Metro Station (Blue Line) | **Hours** Daily 9am – 9pm | **Tip** The National Handicrafts & Handlooms Museum (Bhairon Marg, Pragati Maidan, Tue – Sun 9.30am – 5pm) showcases rural and tribal arts, culture, textiles, and architecture in an immense space.

9 Bagh-e-Bedil

In memory of a great Persian poet

Far away in Afghanistan, the poetry of Bedil is quoted over cups of *chai* by tea sellers in Kabul. While in his adopted country, India, he is lost in the maze of vanishing languages. Called Ghalib's Ghalib by some, criticised as difficult and complicated by others, the Afghani poet Abdul-Qadir Bedil (1642–1720) is remembered only on an occasional evening, organised by those who still speak his tongue.

For many a passerby, this green patch past the Sports Club of India on Mathura Road serves as a sweet respite from the hot haze rising from the tarred road. It has few visitors other than the heat oppressed. The shrine of Hazrat Khwaja Nooruddin, within the same compound, receives more of the faithful.

Forgotten till 2006, Bedil's name grabbed the spotlight when a letter arrived from Tajikistan president Emomali Rahmonov expressing his desire to visit the poet's grave. It was then that the grave was spruced up, and stone tablets with his verses in Tajiki, Persian, Urdu, Hindi, and English were installed.

The green tomb is a topic of debate among scholars. Some believe that his real grave was beside Guzar Ghat in Muhalla Khekariyan, and is now lost, as is Nawab Shukrallah Khan's *haveli* where Bedil lived. Others claim that his followers visited his grave and carried his remains to Afghanistan. Yet another theory talks about a court record that states that Maulana Shah Sulaiman Sahib asked the Nizam Asif Jah VII for funds to restore the Purana Qila grave. It could have been a scam to siphon money, but it's heart-warming to believe otherwise.

For many years, an annual celebration in his name was organised as a cultural event on a grand scale in Shahajanabad. Some days, the Bagh-e-Bedil sees a recital of Bedil's poetry set to *qawwali* (a style of Muslim devotional music). What Bedil would think of *qawwali* – a creation of the poets Ghalib and Aamir Khusro, who he inspired – is anyone's guess.

Address Mathura Road, Pragati Maidan | Getting there Pragati Maidan Metro Station (Blue Line) | Hours Daily, sunrise to sunset | Tip The Supreme Court of India (Tilak Marg, Supreme Court, Mandi House) and other courts are close by.

10__Begumpur Mosque
Delhi's second-largest mosque

From outside, it seems hard to believe that the placid Begumpur Mosque, located next to Malviya Nagar, used to be the largest mosque in Delhi before Shah Jahan constructed Jama Masjid in Chandni Chowk. That is, until you walk up the rough and rubble-covered stone steps through the entrance, which leads to an awe-inspiring large courtyard. An entire village took refuge here in 1739 from marauders of Nadir Shah's army, and the mosque remained occupied by local families until it was evacuated in 1910 when the British started documenting ancient monuments. Later, during the Partition, the mosque again sheltered refugee families, who built brick homes inside, until they too were evacuated. It is still the second-largest mosque in the city.

When Muhammad bin Tughlaq or his successor, Firoz Shah, offered prayers in the courtyard of the mosque during the 1300s, Begumpur would have been considered a splendid structural marvel. The debate over who built the mosque and in exactly which year is a quandary best left to the experts. Despite the severe architectural style with very little ornamentation (peculiar to the Tughlaq era), the grandeur of the mosque is apparent. In its time, the *sehan* or central courtyard, covered by a cloth canopy, would have harboured thousands of *namazis* (worshippers). The cloisters along the sides of the courtyard, with their flowing symmetrical arches, continue to shelter pious devotees; the platforms offer space to siesta-loving residents of the neighbourhood; and the terraces and domes attract intrepid sightseers.

With 64 domes in all, and arches as far as the eye can see, the roof of the mosque becomes an intriguing landscape for any camera-wielding individual. As the sun goes down, young boys enjoy games of cricket on the Sultanate-era pitch. A little further on, a tiny break-dancer entertains his fans, performing on what could be the largest stage in the world.

Address 2, Guru Govind Singh Rd, Begumpur Village | Getting there Haus Khaz Metro Station (Yellow Line) | Hours Daily, sunrise to sunset | Tip The village around the mosque offers a peek into rural life unaffected by urbanisation. Come here for a pleasant amble, especially on a Sunday, while bored horses harnessed to vegetable carts flick their tails impatiently, women dry condiments, and men lounge on *charpoys* (string beds), smoking hookahs and playing cards.

11 Bhairon Mandir
Offer alcohol to the gods

Cartons of the whisky brand Black Dog litter the premises. The unmistakable smell of liquor hits you as you walk down the temple pathway. At most holy places, alcohol and meat are not welcome. At the Bhairon Mandir (as it is commonly known) near Purana Qila, more than a few rules that normally apply to temples are flouted. Here, at the two shrines dedicated to the charismatic god Shiva, polar opposites are revered. One form of Shiva at the Doodhiya Bhairav Temple is appeased by milk. The other, Shiva's fiercest form, Lord Bhairavat, at the Kilkari Bhairav Temple, can only be pleased with alcohol.

Pampered, well-fed, and insolent mutts gambol around the temple compound. Shiva *bhakts* (devotees) will not find it odd because dogs were the vehicles of choice for Lord Shiva. Above the entrance arch are three *chhatris* (cupolas) – the central one covering a Ganesha idol and the other two sheltering two fierce black hounds. Alcohol isn't sold on the premises, so devotees proffer bottles wrapped in black polythene bags to the attendants. The pundits pour some liquor over the head of Bhairava and hand the *prasad* (offerings) back to the devotees.

It is believed that this temple was built on land marking the boundaries of the Pandava palace. And this is one of only five temples in Delhi that dates back to the Mahabharata period. Bhima, the strongest of the Pandavas, is said to have attained his superlative powers meditating here. At the side of the temple, a well called Pandavon ka kuan (Pandavas' Well) is considered holy and beneficial for health. A water dispenser in the shape of a cow, whose udders are fashioned as taps, is bound to get your attention.

The original temple was established during the building of Pandava's city, Indraprastha. The present-day concretised temple is far from its original form, but the energy of the ancient still lingers.

Address Bhairon Mandir, Pragati Maidan | **Getting there** Pragati Maidan Metro Station (Blue Line) | **Hours** Daily 5am–midnight & 3pm–9pm | **Tip** Inside the Purana Qila, the Kunti Devi Temple dedicated to Shiva and Durga, his consort, was also constructed during the era of Pandavas. It is believed to have been built by Kunti, mother of the Pandavas.

12 Bijai Mandal

A hall of a thousand pillars

Captured for posterity by the Moroccan traveller Ibn-e-Batuta, the octagonal citadel of Bijai Mandal lives on in vivid colours in his travelogue. In a dense urban area of Kalu Sarai, very close to a colony called Vijay Mandal, the 14th-century ruins rub shoulders with 21st-century brick buildings. They challenge the ramparts like a bunch of Lilliputians confronting a fallen giant.

The once-splendid court of Sultan Muhammed Tuglaq stands proud, bearing well its collapsed southern section, a crumbling roof, and a hall. In the early 20th century, coins, gold, rubies, and fragments of coral, ivory, and other luxury items were discovered here in two pits during excavation.

Historians have pored over Ibn-e-Batuta's texts ad nauseam to decipher the antecedents of a very debated structure, the Qasr-i-Hazar Sutun, a hall of a thousand pillars. "The pillars are of painted wood, and support a wooden roof, most exquisitely carved. The people sit under this, and it is in this hall that the Sultan sits for public audience," wrote Batuta. Experts debate whether Allauddin Khilji's Hazar Sutun palace and Tuglaq's hall could be the same structure. Pillar bases excavated in 1934 allow for that flight of fancy. An account of a parade of horses, their bridles and girths dressed in black silk; marching troops; and elephants adorned in silk and gold cloths made to bow their heads to the Sultan while chamberlains intermittently cried out, "*Bismillah!*" in praise of the Sultan's absolute power comes to life.

A vista of a heavily guarded fortress where visitors pay customs at several gates to enter the fort-city emerges. The secrets of the Bijai Mandal echo in its grey stones. Young boys scramble to the top of the octagon. In the distance, an old caretaker prays at the grave of 15th-century Sufi saint, Sheikh Hasan Tahir, from the Lodi era. Above the citadel, the wind perhaps still whispers "*Bismillah.*"

Address Kalu Sarai, Begumpur | **Getting there** Haus Khaz Metro Station (Yellow Line) | **Hours** Daily, sunrise to sunset | **Tip** The Aurobindo Ashram (Begumpur Road, Kalu Sarai, Tel +91 11 26567863) with its quiet gardens, is a peaceful retreat that attracts those looking to practice yoga and meditation.

13 _ The Carpet Cellar
The rug kingdom

It all began with one Persian rug that Carpet Cellar founder Sheel Chandra purchased for Rs 200 or 300 in the 1950s. Since then, his collection has grown so large that it is said to rival the collection of the Sultan of Brunei.

Viewed from a comfortable carpet-covered sofa with saddlebag cushions, the store is reminiscent of perfumed oils, elephant caravans, and midnight *mushairas* (poetry recitals). In the absence of a proper carpet museum in the city, this shop opposite Gargi College is the next best thing. Most of the collection is not for public display, but fine reproductions are framed and hung for the viewing pleasure of customers.

Stacks of suzanis, kilins, ikats, and durries are presented with a flourish that almost makes one believe in flying carpets. The space is covered with rugs – between the pillars, up against the walls, and suspended in frames. This is a tactile gallery and visitors are encouraged to touch and feel. Shelves of eco-friendly pashminas, fine *jamadar* shawls, and delicate stoles include heirloom-quality pieces that grandmothers can pass down to the younger generation.

While the oldest carpet in the world, the Pazyryk, found frozen in the ice in Siberia, dates back to the 5th century BC, carpets in India can be traced only to the 15th century. Persian traders schlepped carpets to India long before Emperor Akbar started craft workshops in India. The Carpet Cellar rolls out a plethora of woven works of art, including traditional Persian imports – like the herat, cloudbands, and boteh – and floral masterpieces.

The store offers private workshops where traditional weavers share the nuances of knots and weaves and make the warp and weft come alive. Monthly lectures and exhibitions are available to groups. A new larger, contemporary store is now open at Sultanpur but it is the original Carpet Cellar that is reminiscent of Istanbul souks.

Address 1, Anand Lok, Khel Gaon Marg, Siri Fort Road | **Getting there** Green Park Metro Station (Yellow Line) | **Hours** Daily 10.30am–6.30pm | **Tip** Step out of the Carpet Cellar and into Nature Morte, an exciting contemporary art gallery focusing on emerging Indian artists.

14__Chausanth Khamba

The magic of 64 pillars

An air of perpetual carnival hangs over the lanes of Nizamuddin Basti. The vendors dominate the lanes, peddling steaming snacks of hot *samosas* and *jalebis*, bright colourful clothes, stunning sequined footwear, fresh fruits, delicate bangles, and wares produced to make you haggle.

Amid the crowds and cacophony of horns, an old fort-like gateway reveals an open courtyard of the Urs Mahal, a hall for public celebration. The honking gives way to the cawing of crows and the stillness of the large tree in the centre.

Facing the Urs Mahal, the Chausanth Khamba (circa 1624) can be dismissed as just a wall until you enter the recently restored structure, which also serves as a venue for cultural events and festivals. Deviating from the traditional use of sandstone, this magnificent ode in marble is a wonder of light and shadow. *Chausanth*, meaning 64, is the number of pillars that support 25 bays on which rest 25 inverted domes, making this a unique structure. Don't doubt your math skills if you are able to count only 36 pillars – there's a trick to it.

The Chausanth Khamba was built in the 16th century by Akbar's foster brother, Mirza Aziz Kokaltash, an influential nobleman and the governor of Gujarat. When first constructed, it probably served as a private waiting hall for guests visiting the Urs Mahal celebrations, which would explain its unique architecture. It was later converted into a tomb for Mirza Kokaltash, who died in 1623. Among the unmarked tombs bathed in light, only the identity of his wife's tomb is certain.

In the still of the afternoon, faint voices, the piercing whistle of a pressure cooker, and a boy calling out to his pigeons break the silence. The stone lattice creates patterns of light across the floor, and nothing can disturb this white reverie except perhaps the zealous peacock that has claimed the tomb as its territory.

Address Hazrat Nizamuddin Basti, South District | **Getting there** JLN Stadium Metro Station (Violet Line) | **Hours** Daily 7am–1pm | **Tip** Located nearby is the Mazar-e-Ghalib, the tomb of India's most renowned poet. With its sandstone platform and lattice marble screens, it has been transformed into a poet's *durbar* (court) since its restoration.

15 Chillah Sharif Hazrat Nizamuddin

A divine retreat

Close to Gurdwara Damdama Sahib, and not far from his *dargah* (shrine), is the Chillah Sharif (spiritual retreat) of Hazrat Nizamuddin Auliya, a place where the Auliya and other Sufi masters would come to meditate, fast, and withdraw from the world for 40 days, as prescribed by Sufism. In stark contrast to the chaotic blend of religion, spirituality, and commercialism of the *dargah*, the tree-lined lane leading to this *khanquah* (monastery) retains a serene atmosphere. This place usually does not figure on the tourist trail, and women are not restricted from entering the chambers here.

Only a few believers, seeking blessings and fulfillment of wishes, visit the 13th/14th-century Tughlaq-era walls and chambers. Some pray at the small mosque; others kneel facing the soot-blackened walls of the Auliya's room, now filled with prayer mats and offerings of *chadars* (shrouds), grain, and milk. On the surrounding lawns, writers sit scribbling in notebooks.

The boundary of the original *khanquah* is thought to have extended to Purana Quila, or the Old Fort, and included even Humayun's tomb complex. What remains is a semi-ruin of the original structure. The stones of the *langar khana* (kitchen), *sama khana* (meditation hall), *aam mehfil khana* (gathering hall), and *khas mehfil khana* (private meeting hall) stand as testimony to the devotion of disciple Ziauddin Wakil. He commissioned the *khanquah* despite the Auliya's prediction that whoever built it would die upon its completion. Construction took 30 days, and Wakil died on the last day, while dancing in a *mehfil* (gathering) to celebrate the finished monastery. His body is interred in a graveyard nearby, alongside other followers of the Auliya. On the 5th day after every new moon, there is a special *sama mehfil* with *qawwals* (performers of *qawwali* music) in attendance.

Address Behind the Humayun complex, Mathura Road, Nizamuddin | Getting there
Jangpura Metro Station (Violet Line) / PragatiMadain Metro Station (Blue Line) | Hours
Daily, sunrise to sunset | Tip The Batashewala complex, with three stunning tombs, was
recently restored and is now open for visitors.

16 __ Coronation Durbar Park

A graveyard of British-era statues

More than a century after the British left India, indelible signs of the trading company that once ruled over princely states forced to accede to the sovereign authority of the crown still remain. One such place is the Coronation Durbar Park, or Coronation Memorial, in north Delhi at Burari Road. Today, this surreal remnant of the past and the memory of a *durbar* (court or audience) hailing foreign rulers seem almost preposterous. The fact that it is so far away from the bustling centre of the town adds to the incongruity of the grand *durbars* that took place here, thrice.

The first *durbar* was in 1877, when Queen Victoria was proclaimed Empress of India; the second in 1905, to announce the anointment of Edward VII; and the last grand *durbar* was in 1911, where the newly crowned King-Emperor George V announced that India's capital would be shifted from Kolkata (Calcutta) to Delhi. The memorial has been in the making for years. The huge metal gates are held together with loose chains, and if you try, you can slip in through a gap.

A huge obelisk at the centre of the park looms over the surrounding flat land. It is installed at the exact location of the king and the queen's announcement of the decision to move the capital. Children run through the fountains created by ruptures in the pipes that water the vegetation of this schizophrenic landscape, one half covered by manicured lawns, the other half dry and arid. Statues of English noblemen and kings stand amid vacant sandstone plinths around the obelisk. In one corner, a playground with a jungle gym and swings adds a sense of dissonance to the historic setting. In a way, the time-ravaged statues of George V, Lord Hardinge, Sir John Jenkins, Sir Guy Fleetwood Wilson, and the Marquess of Willingdon, a nose lopped off on one and a crow perched on another, seem to simultaneously glorify and mock the empire that once was.

Address Shanti Swaroop Tyagi Marg, near Nirankari Sarovar, Model Town | Getting there Vishwavidyalaya Metro Station (Yellow Line) | Hours Mon–Sat 10am–8pm | Tip Next door to the park, the Sant Nirankari Mission's Fountain of Oneness in Nirankari Sarovar complex attracts a crowd on most evenings. Visitors can experience a music, light, and water show at 6.30pm every Friday, Saturday, and Sunday.

17 __ Dar-e-Shikoh Library
A Mughal prince's library

The Shahzada-e-Buland Iqbal ("Prince of High Fortune"), as declared by his father, was anything but fortunate in his life. He died a dishonourable death, slaughtered in front of his second-born by his own brother Aurangzeb. Yet his memory lives on as a tribute to man's honourable pursuit of knowledge, no matter the cost.

The strong opposition that Prince Dara Shikoh faced over the throne was mainly due to his liberal beliefs, which threatened his orthodox brothers. His philosophy binding the beauty of Islam with the esoteric faiths of India made him a danger to the Mughal regime, according to dissenters. Nevertheless, his legacy endures beyond the game of thrones. His translation of the *Upanishads*, the philosophical basis for Hinduism, was his last work, completed in 1657. It was this Persian version, *Sirri-i-Akbar*, that the West discovered first, and not the Sanskrit original.

The Dar-e-Shikoh Library's Qutb Khana, at Ambedkar University, (now without books) remains a symbol of the prince's intellectual curiosity. It was once a repository of a priceless collection of translated Persian and Sanskrit texts, European books, and rare manuscripts. The premises, which over time have changed hands many times, are now used by the Archaeological Survey of India. After Dara Shikoh's death, the Qutb Khana was given to the nobleman Ali Mardaan. It finally housed David Ochterlony, the first British resident. The Greek-style colonnades with grey-blue shutters are a visible British alteration to the sandstone Mughal-era building – the latter only visible when you see the *baradaris* (corridors) still intact behind the additions.

A tiny musty museum run by the archaeology department on the premises has some pottery and artefacts on display. It has been the venue for cultural festivals, theatre groups, storytellers, and artists. Dar-e-Shikoh, the erudite prince, lives on through these endeavours.

Address Ambedkar University, Lothian Road, Kashmere Gate | Getting there Kashmere
Gate Metro Station (Red/Yellow Line) | Hours Mon–Sat 10am–5pm | Tip The calm
Nicholson Cemetery (Club Road, Civil Lines) on the tourist trail is a well-maintained
counterpoint to the Lothian Cemetery. The graves are mostly of fallen British soldiers
from the 1857 Uprising, a reminder of a brutal past.

18__Daryaganj Book Market

Where the streets are paved with books

A typical Sunday morning for bibliophiles of Delhi begins at around 10 o'clock on the streets of Daryaganj. Starting from Hotel Broadway and stretching all the way to the main market, booksellers flood the pavements with yellowing dog-eared volumes for sale. This is the Daryaganj Sunday market, where a veritable cornucopia is on offer for bargain hunters and rare-book aficionados alike.

This could be called an open-air temple of books. It is also one of the rare places where you will see sellers step on their merchandise, an act considered taboo in India as books are revered as the abode of Saraswati, the goddess of learning. Bargain hunters will shove and push to lay their hands on a find. A pair of hawk eyes is essential to seek out that elusive book, comic, graphic novel, collector's edition, or international imprint you won't find at bookstores. It could even be a title that doesn't sell in the country. Vendors glide over books to get to the copy you point at.

The market has dodged many a bullet. Over the years, attempts have been made to relocate it because of the traffic snarls it creates. Intellectuals, journalists, and academics who frequent the weekly affair have thwarted these efforts. With books that retail for hundreds of rupees available for just Rs 50 and Rs 100, loyalists are willing to go to any lengths to protect this treasure trove.

The market offers an eclectic choice of subjects, ranging from the Hindu Pantheon to a book about Indian plants and their Ayurvedic uses. Rare editions dating back to the 18th century aren't uncommon. But the most precious gem you will find at Daryaganj is a bookseller who will gauge your literary pulse, dive into the stacks, and pull out a book you never knew existed. The magic of discovery is still alive at this market.

Address Near Delite Cinema, Daryaganj | **Getting there** New Delhi Metro Station (Yellow Line) | **Hours** Sun 10am–6pm | **Tip** Stop in for lunch at Moti Mahal (3703, Netaji Subhash Marg, Daryaganj), the restaurant where butter chicken was born.

19__Dastkar Nature Bazaar
The alternative Dilli Haat

The air is carnival-esque at the Dastkar Nature Bazaar. For those in the know, Dastkar's stalls are a treasure trove of imperfectly beautiful handicrafts. Forgotten artistries relegated to the far corners of the country have been given pride of place at Dastkar's intermittent exhibitions, organised in major cities. Now, Dastkar has a regular, permanent space at Andheria Modh. The Dastkar Nature Bazaar, in collaboration with Delhi Tourism, has brought the craft market to a space that was formerly a *Kisan Haat* (farmers market).

The atmosphere is reminiscent of a village market, except the stalls are decked with wares from all over India. Spread across 7,000 square feet, the redbrick booths with bamboo barriers host a permanent bazaar for eco-friendly products. Here, colourful patchwork quilts and one-of-a-kind hand-loomed saris vie for attention; naturally dyed *shibori* apparel competes with *leheriya dupattas* (stoles tie-dyed in wavelike patterns). Whether *Mata-ni-pachedi* saris, *ikat* cushions, or handcrafted stoneware, each item brings hundreds of years of history within the reach of urbanites. The makers of these one-of-a-kind products take great pride in explaining the warp and weft to jubilant shoppers.

Dastkar's themed surprises involve green bazaars, festival specials, summer weaves, crafts from the Northeast, and arts from West Bengal. There is always something new – either a folk singer or a musician performing, or *beherupiyas* (roving disguised actors) showcasing a vanishing art. Couples buy knickknacks for new homes. Children spin handmade tops or play hide-and-seek using the colourful cut-outs near the stalls as shields. The aromas of well-curated regional food draw in hungry families.

It's a day well spent discovering the rich plethora of arts and crafts from across the country. This is a carnival that will give you a hangover of the rustic kind.

Address Nature Bazaar, Kisan Haat, Anuvrat Marg, Andheria Modh, Chhatarpur, www.dastkar.org, info@dastkar.org, Tel +91 11 26808633 | **Getting there** Chhattarpur Metro Station (Yellow Line) | **Hours** Daily 11am–8pm | **Tip** Look out for artisans offering to teach the basic skills of quilling, papier-mâché, thread jewellery, pottery, and painting styles like *pichwai* (painted cloth) and botanical art.

20__Delhi 6
The royal sport of pigeon handling

Old Delhi, or its more cinematic name Delhi 6 (the area pin code), is an acquired taste. This slice of Delhi, also called the walled city, romantic as it sounds, is no Roman Pantheon, nor is it a cobbled city quarter or a perfumed palace. The teeming streets will overwhelm you, the dust will hurt your eyes, and the hot sun will make you want to retreat to your cosy room. But if you persist and walk around the Jama Masjid and Matia Mahal area, and look up to the skies, you will witness one of Old Delhi's cherished pastimes – *kabutarbazi* (pigeon handling).

Although hobbyist pigeon handlers are many, *khalifas* and *ustads*, who are renowned masters in the art of pigeon-flying, are rare finds. Pigeon-flying is a hobby that every old-city resident has indulged in at one time or another. Pigeon coops on rooftops house pampered birds that are fed dry fruits and special feed that cost *lakhs* (hundreds of thousands) of rupees. The practice has even led to the financial ruin of many families here. The sport finds its roots in the royal tradition of keeping and training homing pigeons that would fly several thousand kilometres carrying messages. Today, it involves flying either an individual pigeon or *girebaz* (flock). The birds that fly the longest are declared winners. *Tugudi* is when two or more handlers release their flocks simultaneously and the flocks return bringing other pigeons along.

Find a spot where you won't be trampled, and when your curiosity gets the better of you, ask the shopkeepers, who will usher you to a nearby roof, or even invite you to a cousin's friend's place. Amid tangled wires, dilapidated buildings, and open gutters, on the rooftops you will experience the madness of this sport with thousands of pigeons and a few kites overhead. Follow the whirling handkerchiefs, shouting, whistling, and calls, and you are sure to find yourself in the thick of things.

Address Matia Mahal, Near Jama Masjid | **Getting there** Chawri Bazaar Metro Station (Yellow Line) | **Hours** It's a spring/winter sport to be played in the evenings when the skies are clear. For easy access, you can also contact reputed guides for an organised pigeon-handling experience. | **Tip** On 26 January, it is a tradition for pigeon handlers to participate in a huge sporting event that is announced through flyers and word of mouth (and lately, Facebook).

21 Delhi Blue Pottery Trust

The birthplace of Indian studio pottery

The basement, right at the corner of an unassuming apartment block, is an unlikely location for a pottery studio. In a quiet lane of Safdarjung, India's oldest pottery school is busy shaping the next generation of artists. To understand the name Delhi Blue, one has to travel back in time. The blue glaze-tiled monuments were the first exposure that the British had to Persian pottery. They didn't know it was an ancient process that travelled from Egypt through Persia, and then to India with the Mughals. The name Delhi Blue stuck and was adopted by Gurcharan Singh, the father of the studio pottery movement in India.

This love of pottery and the transformation of the utilitarian into an art form can be attributed to the passion of Singh. In the 1920s, a freshly enthused Singh who had spent considerable time learning at the potter's wheel in Japan returned to India. He began researching clay under the patronage of the Maharaja of Bundi. Later, along with Abdullah Mussalman – a descendent of the Pathan potters famous for creating the blue glaze visible on Mughal monuments in Delhi – he set up the Delhi Blue Pottery Trust.

A stairway leads you to the basement and into a tiny room filled with notices, art exhibition brochures, and posters. Next, a narrow passage opens onto a large exposed brick area, where diffused light reveals a clutter of wheels, pots, and raw materials. At one end, students concentrate on shaping a lump of clay at their wheel. An instructor constructively comments on what could be done with a lopsided vase. This is no art gallery, but the studio offers classes to serious students only. At the wood-fired kiln, there's a hush of expectation among a group of students who wait to see what heat might have done to their delicately shaped clay. At the other end, rows and rows of earthenware stand as testament to the enduring magic of pottery.

Address Delhi Blue Apartments, Safdarjang Ring Road, www.delhibluepotterytrust.com, infodbpt@yahoo.co.in, Tel +91 11 26190223 | Getting there AIIMS Metro Station (Yellow Line) | Hours By appointment, Mon–Sat 11am–6pm | Tip Safdarjung's tomb (Safdarjung Road and Aurobindo Marg intersection) built in the 17th century is similar in design to Humayun's tomb but lacks in refinement. It was built using material stripped from Abdur-Rahim Khan-i-Khana's tomb.

22 Delhi College of Art
Finding Queen Victoria

Around the world, statues of the British monarchy still grace public spaces of the former empire's liberated colonies. In India too, a few reminders of the Raj still serve as historic landmarks. However, Delhi, the city built to be the capital of the British Empire in India, has just one statue of Queen Victoria. And only a select few know where it exists. It used to be on the pedestal outside the Delhi Town Hall in Chandni Chowk until just after Independence. Now, the sombre statue of nationalist hero and educationist Swami Shraddananda has replaced the old guard. Today, the queen rests in the much gentler surroundings of the Delhi College of Art.

In the 1960s, Delhi's British-era statues and monuments were removed from their pedestals and relegated to the Coronation Park (see p. 40). With nationalistic fervour at its peak, the Queen Victoria statue was vandalised, resulting in its being moved to its current location.

The bronze statue of the woman who ruled the Indian sub-continent for 63 years sits to the left of the first pathway into the building complex. The statue of the queen, seated on a throne, was made in 1857 to mark her position as the Empress of India. A modest gate on a broad avenue leads to the artistic campus, where installations, sculptures, and artists pepper the sylvan surroundings. The contemporary brick architecture juxtaposed against students' works of art makes for a striking setting.

The queen looks slightly despondent about being relegated to the corner where she can only lord over a *semal* (silk cotton) tree that rewards her with fiery red buds. Sculptor Alfred Turner, who was commissioned to create three bronze statues of the queen after receiving global acclaim for his "Fishergirl," would probably approve of the fact that budding artists are sketching his statue. It isn't part of their coursework though, and some of the students only know the statue as the "foreign lady."

Address 20–22, Tilak Marg, Mandi House | Getting there Mandi House Metro Station (Blue/Violet Line) | Hours Mon–Fri 9am–5pm (except national holidays) | Tip The Bengali Market, near a traffic circle, is one of the oldest markets in Delhi. Nathu's Sweets and Bengali Sweet House are all-time favourites, and their confections and snacks are a must-indulge (23–25, Bengali Market, Connaught Place, 10am–11pm).

23___Delhi Eye

India's largest Ferris wheel

In an amusement and water park close to Noida, a 200-foot-high Ferris wheel, inspired by the London Eye and Singapore Flyer, offers head-spinning views of the capital city. This is a far cry from the usual giant-wheel experience in India, which usually entails a thrill ride on a bare wooden seat with just a bar preventing you from falling off. Each of the 36 air-conditioned glass pods of the Delhi Eye holds up to eight passengers. As with its London counterpart, the sound volume, light, and music can be controlled inside the pods.

The fifth-largest Ferris wheel in the world spins in really slow circles, allowing passengers to take in the leisurely view of the river Yamuna that spreads below. The ride lasts 20 minutes, during which the wheel completes three rotations.

There's even a luxury pod that comes with plush couches, a champagne cooler, a television screen with a DVD player (in case you prefer watching a movie that lasts 20 minutes), and a phone connected to the control room. If all of this becomes overwhelming, a panic button is fitted within each pod. Fortunately, there has never been an occasion for its use.

As the wheel slowly moves up, enthusiastic spectators from the water park below cheer and wave. The view of the Yamuna, though covered in hyacinth, is exhilarating. Spotting historical monuments like Red Fort, Humayun's Tomb, the Lotus Temple, the Akshardham Temple, and the Qutb Minar becomes a game of sorts. Eagle-eyed passengers can see not only the monuments but also Connaught Place on a clear day. This joyride gives one the feeling of being at the highest point in Delhi. It is a novel experience, as there are only a few skyscrapers in the city centre. Besides the Delhi Eye, the park, spread over three acres, offers several rides, a gaming zone, 6D theatre, and food courts – enough to keep a family busy for an entire day.

Address Kalindi Kunj Road, Kalindi Kunj Park, Okhla Block H, Shaheen Bagh, Jasola Vihar, www.delhirides.in, delhirides@gmail.com, Tel +91 11 64659291 | **Getting there** Jasola (Apollo) Metro Station (Violet Line) | **Hours** Daily 11am–8pm. Tickets: Rs 30 | **Tip** Nature enthusiasts can head to the Okhla Bird Sanctuary (Gautam Buddh Nagar, Noida, Uttar Pradesh) between 7.30am and 5pm to spot a large variety of water birds like the rare bar-headed goose, cormorants, jacamas, and moorhens, among others. The sanctuary is approachable from Mathura Road (NH-2), via Sarita Vihar, going towards Noida.

24___Delhi Ivory Palace

An embroidery museum in a 300-year-old shop

The legendary riches of Old Delhi live on its bazaars. The Delhi Ivory Palace is one shop that has seen Shahjanabad through centuries of change. Its weathered wooden façade bears a signboard that harks back to a time when ivory was a prized (and legal) possession. Established as Messrs Faqir Chand Raghunath Dass, it attracted the finest craftsmen of its day. The Mughal Sultanate, European travellers, and resident British officers' penchant for Asian artwork, jewellery, and ivory made Delhi's Ivory Palace a very popular destination. Inside, a wall in an inner room displays old newspaper cuttings featuring heads of state, dignitaries, and even the Beatles visiting the store. Their remarks in the registry are a testimony to the establishment's erstwhile legacy.

With the ban on ivory in force, another signboard, slung so high up that one could easily miss it, now pronounces this to be the Museum of Embroidery. At the entrance, a skilled craftsman seated on a cushioned platform meditates over his intricate needlework. His fingers move deftly, coaxing a pattern out of copper and gold thread. A resplendent large peacock motif by award-winning artisan Sheikh Shamsuddin dominates the interior. The display case is peppered with Asian-style art pieces, and none of them are for sale.

In a labyrinthine arrangement of glass shelves, heirloom jewellery pieces vie with bejewelled embroidered clutches. Delicately carved rosewood screens, antique chairs, old-style cabinets, and ebony frames with miniature paintings give the shop the bearing of a vintage museum.

An old photograph shows an ivory sofa set that is no longer on display. Intended as gifts for Queen Victoria, the furnishings depicted took the craftsmen, a father-son duo, 27 years to complete. This is the closest and the best impression of Ali Baba's cave of treasures.

Address 1080, Northern Gate, Jama Masjid Road, Jama Masjid, Chandni Chowk, www.ivorypalaceindia.com | Getting there Chawri Bazar Metro Station (Yellow Line) | Hours Mon–Sat 10am–8pm | Tip The Indraprastha Girls' School (1051, Pai Walan, behind Jama Masjid) was Delhi's first all-girls school. A stamp to commemorate its 100-year anniversary was released by the Indian post in 2006. European arched doorways, stained-glass windows, and a central hall with a fireplace are some of the features of the 19th-century structure.

25 Delhi Metro Museum

South Asia's first modern metro museum

Delhi Metro is like a decongestant that has opened up the stuffy sinuses of an ancient city. The city's subterranean transport system has changed the landscape of what was perceived as Delhi. It has woven together the fabric of the city that once was a scattering of embassies, monuments, urban colonies, and rural pockets. Set up in a span of just two months in 2010, the Delhi Metro Museum is an attempt to present the making of this public transport system.

At Patel Chowk Metro Station, the upper level is an ode to the stable of metal steeds that has become the lifeline of millions. The first thing that greets the eye is a replica of the metro system's control room. The temptation to either sit in the control room or touch the panels is deterred with the stern message: "Don't touch the exhibits." Children clamour over Metro ties, pens, and key chains at the souvenir shop. For adults, the most coveted piece of merchandise is the Metro model train.

A display recounting the construction of Chawri Bazar Metro Station's mammoth building offers a glimpse into what it is like to pierce the heart of Delhi's most ancient city. The solution was to go deep. In fact, this is the second-deepest Metro station in the world. This makes it worth spending a few minutes at the information panel of the impressive tunnel-boring machine. A handcrafted model of the metro car takes pride of place. Unsurprisingly, it is this exhibit that attracts the most attention, as do the ungainly mannequins beside it that showcase the various uniforms of the Metro workers.

A few documentary-style photographs chronicling and feting the champions of the Delhi Metro record the developmental phases of the massive project. The real story behind this gargantuan effort is perhaps best revealed in the series of monochrome images of its unsung heroes: the Metro labourers.

Address Patel Chowk Metro Station, Janpath, Connaught Place, www.delhimetrorail.com/metro-museum.aspx | Getting there Patel Chowk Metro Station (Yellow Line) | Hours Daily 10am–11pm | Tip De Paul's (22, Janpath Bhawan, Janpath), a Delhi favourite, is a small eatery that sells the best cold coffee in Delhi. There is always a crowd clamouring for snacks, sandwiches, and a house brew of bottled cold coffee.

26 __ Delhi Police Headquarters
The country's tallest mural

How did a couple of artists convince the Delhi police to allow them to paint a mural on their headquarters wall? They simply made an offer that the Delhi police couldn't refuse, or rather chose a subject no Indian could say no to. At 158 feet, the black-and-white painting of Mahatma Gandhi, beaming over the city's busiest intersection – the ITO Crossing – is India's tallest mural, and arguably the most inspiring. Artists Hendrik Beikirch and Anpu Varkey took a mere five days to complete the piece, using an aerial lift. Its official unveiling on Martyr's Day (the anniversary of Mahatma Gandhi's death) on January 30, 2014 proved to be just as apt.

This traffic-stopper has a calming effect on rushing vehicles, which slow down just a tad to take in the sight. With its nuanced details – from the soft creases in his white shawl to the lines tracing the craggy much-adored face, the mural is perhaps the most unique tribute honouring the great leader. Even the grain of the wall lends a distinctive texture to the larger-than-life bespectacled figure. For Indians, this image is a nostalgic reminder of the many black-and-white newsreels in which they have seen the "Father of the Nation" inspiring millions.

For ECB (the name by which Hendrik is popular in the art world), who normally paints portraits of fictional characters, Gandhi's mural is one of the few exceptions. Busan, the second-largest city in South Korea, plays host to the "Fisherman," ECB's largest mural in Asia, standing at 238 feet. Anpu, who assisted ECB, is famous as the *billi* (cat) lady. She is the artist behind the popular piece of street art in the city's Shahpur Jat (see p. 128) area. ECB's monochromatic murals on concrete walls across cities in America, Russia, Britain, Sweden, Brazil, Denmark, and now India are his way of reminding us of our common humanity – a belief shared by the Mahatma.

Address Indraprastha Marg, IP Estate | **Getting there** Pragati Maidan Metro Station (Blue Line) | **Hours** Daily, sunrise to sunset | **Tip** To escape the unceasing traffic outside, head to the Abdul Nabi Mosque nearby, which has been resurrected as the Jamiat Ulema-i-Hind (Organization of Indian Islamic Scholars). The beautiful courtyard is an unexpected oasis in the centre of chaos. Jamiat was one of the few organisations that did not align with the Muslim League in its demand for a separate nation.

27__Delhi's Barsatis
The penthouse charm

Beyond the monuments, tawdry nightclubs, and glitzy malls, there is a Delhi of colonies, *tankis* (water tanks), and *barsatis* (rooftop dwellings). These last comprise Delhi's creative solution to the problem of space and a loophole around tenancy contracts. As the cheapest rental option, they have served as the go-to quarters for the city's transient population.

Barsatis originated as shelters from unpredictable rains for Delhi families sleeping on rooftop terraces during balmy summers. From tin sheds they evolved into constructed rooms, often used to store things or as living quarters for single relatives or visiting guests. Delhiites have fond memories of spending childhood afternoons in the seclusion of *barsatis*. They also serve as an empowering tool for today's younger generation, giving them space and independence. Many artists and writers have celebrated these spaces through their works.

Today, they are a part of Delhi's DNA. A *barsati* is often the first home for many young couples just starting out. Students from out of town, artists, journalists, and musicians opt for the convenience it provides. The last group has elevated the *barsati's* status to a creative abode. Architect Ameet Singh designed his *barsati* (pictured opposite) as his oasis. On a warm day he enjoys the scent of mandarin oranges, the calls of rare birds, and the sight of his sunken garden. It is his way of being close to nature. Living in a *barsati* exposes you to the elements – not just heat, cold, and dust, but also the breeze and open air.

With Delhi's building trends changing, the *barsati's* latest incarnation is as a boutique hotel. The Lazy Patio in Hauz Khas Village offers travellers a plush *barsati* experience. Restaurants like Potbelly in Shahpur Jat and Cafe Turtle are gen-next versions of the old *barsati*. For some places are not just about an address, but about a vibe.

Address The Lazy Patio, 22 Hauz Khas Village, 4th floor. There are also online expat groups and real-estate listings that you can look up to request a barsati viewing. | **Getting there** Hauz Khas Metro Station (Yellow Line) | **Tip** The Potbelly Rooftop Cafe (116 C, 4th floor, Shahpur Jat) and Cafe Turtle (Shop 23, 1st & 2nd floors, Khan Market), both offer a great view, a hearty meal, and a boho ambience, bringing you as close to the *barsati* experience as is commercially possible.

28__Delite Theatre

Delhi's best cinema experience

On its opening night, the first movie to play at Delite Theatre – *Angaarey*, starring Raj Kapoor – received less attention than it normally would. The newsprint chatter was more about the most luxurious theatre in the city.

Cinemas are at the heart of India's cities. For most, they bring back the youthful nostalgia of playing hooky to watch movies all day. In the middle of Daryaganj, an Old Delhi neighbourhood, Delite happens to be one of the first post-Independence theatres. As you walk down the heritage corridor, a reminder of the movie hall's glorious past is on display. Photographs of leaders like Jawaharlal Nehru and Indira Gandhi share space with those of the great cine-stars of the 1950s and 1970s, like Madhubala, Nutan, and Sunil Dutt.

On April 30, 1954, when Delite opened its doors, it was the tallest building in town. Brij Mohan Lal Raizada, a big movie buff, erected this grand 1,100-seat high-tech extravaganza on the most expensive real estate in Delhi at the time. Being the first air-conditioned theatre in North India only earned it more brownie points in the brutal summers of the plains. Today, Delite straddles a fine balance between a single-screen-theatre experience and multiplex service, with Delite Diamond.

The plush lobby, cool marble interiors, and imported chandeliers are all part of the theatre's elegant ambiance. The crown in Delite Diamond, a handpainted crimson dome tinged with blue, envelops patrons, making them feel like royalty for a few hours. The charm of old-world luxury is taken a notch higher, with brocade chairs and brass cup holders. And single-screen theatre fans will love the balcony, an almost extinct space in the age of multiplexes. On a sweltering afternoon, Delite, with its *maha* (mega) samosas, plush marble restrooms, and original perfume dispensers is the most delightful place to be in Delhi.

Address Asaf Ali Marg, Daryaganj, www.delitecinemas.com, Tel +91 11 23272903 |
Getting there Rajiv Chowk Metro Station (Yellow Line) | **Tip** Chor Bizarre is a Kashmiri
restaurant with a 1927 Fiat roadster as the talking point. Odd bits of furniture and decor
elements simulate a thieves' market.

29__Devi Art Foundation
Breathing life into contemporary Indian art

Right in the heart of Gurgaon, just ahead of Gold Souk restaurant, the striking structure of the Devi Art Foundation sets itself apart from the concretised grid from the first glimpse. Within the stark building, major works ranging from paintings and sculptures to videos and photographs find an artful home. This 7,500-square-foot gallery is probably the first contemporary art space that isn't geared towards commercial displays. Devi Art Foundation brings the aesthetic vision of businessman Anupam Poddar and his mother, Lekha Poddar, to fruition. The Lekha and Anupam Collection is considered one of the most comprehensive private contemporary art collections in the country.

The post-industrial warehouse-style architecture of the gallery space itself is a work of art. The corroded steel façade and its deep rust colour are a striking contrast to the bright blue sky, and the interplay of shadow and sunlight on the burnt-sienna bricks changes throughout the day. Poured cement floors, high ceilings, and exposed beams encourage the viewer to focus on the art. The collapsible wall partitions, designed to adapt to current exhibits, and swaying walkways connecting the galleries make the space an interactive experience.

Themed exhibitions explore contemporary artistic expressions and inspire conversation. Their inaugural exhibit, *Still Moving Image*, in 2008, featured the mediums of photography, film, and video. Since then, the centre has played host to acclaimed displays such as *Where in the World*, which examined the relationship of contemporary Indian artists with the international art world; and *Resemble/Reassemble*, a survey of contemporary art from Pakistan. The foundation organises lectures and workshops that introduce its audience to global yet familiar art. Tugging at invisible strings, this is one place that promises a different experience with every visit.

Address Sirpur House, Plot No. 39, Sector 44, Gurgaon, www.deviartfoundation.org, info@deviartfoundation.org, Tel +91 124 4888177 | **Getting there** HUDA Metro Station (Yellow Line) | **Hours** Tue–Sun 11am–9pm | **Tip** Kingdom of Dreams (Auditorium Complex, Sector 29, Gurgaon), an entertainment concept, brings live Bollywood musicals to the stage. It has a variety of shops, cafes, and restaurants. Culture Gully is a major draw for stalls that showcase street food from all the Indian states.

30__Devi Prasad Sadan Dhobi Ghat

A dhobi ghat in the centre of the city

A *dhobi's* (washerman's) natural workplace is the bank of a river, literally beating the dirt out of clothes at a *ghat* (a stairway down to the water). Among the high-rises of Connaught Place, in a tranquil lane with washing lines on both sides, remains one of the few traditional *dhobi ghats* of Delhi. It is quaint that in the age of washing machines and laundromats, the Devi Prasad Sadan Dhobi Ghat continues to function as it has since the 1970s. When the government shut down laundries near Gole Market and Karol Bagh, a few families traditionally involved in the trade re-established their business here.

In a small courtyard, industrious men whirl sheets into the air, bringing them down on a flogging stone with a resounding slap, resulting in a spray of water and detergent. The place is strewn with washing paraphernalia. Resembling bathtubs, the *chilamchis*, or cement basins, are used for soaking clothes. Water tanks, where all the tumbling, beating on stone, and wringing is done, surround these tubs.

The neighbouring open space is strewn with bedsheets, curtains, and clothes on makeshift lines, which are zealously guarded by a dog that takes its job (very) seriously. It is apt that this meditative, backbreaking washing process concludes with folding and sorting at the shrine dedicated to Nagarsen Baba Ghatwale, the god of the *ghats*.

The grey building next door is home to the 64 families that have lived and worked together since relocation. The facilities are shared, but most *dhobis* work independently, providing services mainly to ministers, hospitals, and hotels. Bring your laundry here and they will be happy to discuss stains and treatment, peppered with some history of their community. The third generation seems to be moving away from the trade, though.

Address Hailey Road, Vakil Lane, Connaught Place | **Getting there** Barakhamba Road
Metro Station (Blue Line) | **Hours** Daily 9am–5pm | **Tip** Next door to the *dhobi ghat*,
the Agrasen or Ugrasen ki Baoli has become a major attraction with tourists after being
featured as the temporary home of the character Aamir Khan plays in the movie *PK*.

31__Dhoomimal Art Gallery
The cradle of Delhi's contemporary art scene

In 1935, Dhoomimal Dharamdas Stationers and Printers was one of the first shops to move from Katra Neel in Chandni Chowk to Connaught Place, the stately new market with its coliseum design. Most business concerns there catered to diplomats, bureaucrats, and officers. A few, like Dhoomimal's founder, Ram Chand Jain, brought with them an existing customer base. A budding, and mostly struggling community of Indian artists patronised the shop and would often barter paintings for art supplies. Ram Babu started displaying the work of his close friends at his store, in the process laying the foundation for one of the oldest art galleries in India.

Today the boulevards don't have British officers and *memsahibs* (wives) with parasols browsing the shops. Next door to the gallery, a Starbucks entertains a young and upwardly mobile demographic. In an age of swanky interiors, the plain, split-level space of Dhoomimal retains an unpretentious air. Now considered small by modern standards, the gallery has seen some of the most vibrant soirees of the art world. Since 2014, Dhoomimal's renovated courtyard has been hosting an art *haat* (market) every Wednesday evening, introducing a new fount of artists like Amrita Ghosh, alongside veteran artists like Bimal Das Gupta.

The vibe is of explorers charting a new artscape, one where art is interactive, approachable, and affordable. Mingling with contemporary art connoisseurs in the small rectangular courtyard, it's not difficult to imagine works of stalwarts like Jamini Roy, M. F. Hussain, F. N. Souza, and Jogen Chowdhury being introduced here in a different era and being received with similar anticipation and excitement.

Director Uday Jain and his mother, Uma Jain, can be found on most days in the small office, planning the next art event, offering the country's talent a fitting platform to reach their audience.

Address G42, Connaught Place, Outer Circle, www.dhoomimalgallery.com, info@dhoomimalartgallery.com | **Getting there** Rajiv Chowk Station (Blue & Yellow Lines) | **Hours** Mon–Sat 11am–6:30pm. Art market every Wednesday evening. Check with the gallery for a schedule. | **Tip** A newer offshoot of the gallery, the Dhoomimal Art Centre (A 8, Connaught Place), hosts art retrospective exhibits regularly.

32 Embassy of Belgium

One of the 20th century's 1,000 best buildings

To an untrained eye, the sprawling Belgian embassy complex may appear like a collection of hollow pillars resembling a large church organ. Some might see glimpses of Mughal architectural style in it, while others may liken it to a set of igloos. This ambiguity is something that pleases its designer, artist-painter-sculptor Satish Gujral. He was awarded the Order of the Crown by Belgium for his architecture.

Completed in the 1980s, the fort-like structure, covered in green climbers and framed by manicured lawns, exudes a calm, pleasant dignity. Despite its function as a public office building it has a private feel, and in its centre hides a cul-de-sac designed in the *vada* or *baramda* style. The deep verandas, quirky stairways, and multiple levels add a textural feel to the entire composition. Its form makes it evident that Gujral did not set out to construct a building but to sculpt one. The cupolas inside are a source of natural light illuminating the plush marble interiors.

The complex is divided into four functional areas spread over five acres of land. The main chancery block holds the offices and a chancellor's house, while the resident ambassador's private home, along with his house staff's living quarters, is around the back. Security issues (it is an embassy, after all) put severe restrictions on exploring this evocative structure, but some areas are open to visitors.

This Indian interpretation of modern architecture pays homage to Indus Valley civilisation in its use of material. It has elements of Mughal style woven in, and in a rare departure, steers clear of colonial influences. Gujral is not a proponent of the "form follows function" adage. His unconventional approach has led to this unique, organic creation. There isn't any question, then, as to why the Belgian embassy was named by the International Forum of Architects as one of the 20th century's 1,000 best buildings.

Address 50-N, Shantipath, Chanakyapuri | Getting there Race Course Metro Station (Yellow Line) | Hours Mon–Fri 9am–12pm. Entry is restricted to some parts. | Tip The National Rail Museum (Shanti Path, Chanakyapuri) tempts even adults to act like children, with a fun-filled mini choo-choo ride and interesting train memorabilia.

33 Feroz Shah Kotla Fort
Meet the affable letter-reading djinns

Any other day of the week, the Feroz Shah Kotla Fort looks like an aging, benevolent protector of squirrels, butterflies, and pigeons from the kites circling above. But come Thursday, the alcoves of the ruins open their arms to visitors, ready to accept the offerings they bring. William Dalrympyle's *City of Djinns* doffs a hat to this phenomenon, portraying Delhi as a city that brims with a multitude of these celestial, mystical beings, thanks to its war-riddled history and its cultural roots in Sufism.

Thursdays are when the *djinns* (spirits) take in requests and hear the pleas of harried souls. The scents of crushed rose petals and incense imbue the walls of the fort. Families make offerings, and pin up photocopies of requests for the recovery of ailing loved ones, for mental stability, for money or marriage, and even for success on college entrance exams. The sooty chambers below the 13-metre-high Ashokan pillar, erected in the 3rd century BC, are decorated by visitors with coloured powder and lamps. Around the pillar, threads and letters are tied to the grills to appease Laatwale Baba, the resident *djinn*. The derelict Jami Masjid within the fort and the stepwell are the only places excluded from this ritual.

Some believe that this letter-writing tradition started when a *fakir* (ascetic), Laddo Shah, took up residence in the fort during the political emergency of 1975–77. Another theory is that during the reign of Mohammad bin Tughlaq, a cruel ruler, oppressed subjects hurled abuse-filled letters into his council chamber at night. After his death, his successor, Feroz Shah, sought messages of forgiveness from those who his predecessor had wronged and placed them in his tomb. Finding reason in an intangible experience seems inconsequential in the glow of lamps, as you watch peaceful families enjoy their meals knowing that the *djinns* will be reading their deepest desires.

Address Bahadur Shah Zafar, Balmiki Basti, Vikram Nagar | Getting there Indraprastha or Pragati Maidan Metro Station (Blue Line) | Hours Daily, sunrise to sunset. Admission fee: Free on Thu, other days Rs 100 for foreigners. | Tip The Khooni Darwaza, or Bloody Door, is five minutes down the road. From the days of the Sultanate to as recently as 1947, when the British partitioned India, this gateway has seen ordered killings, murders, and massacres. Rumours that it is haunted gain strength during the monsoon season, when the gateway looks as if blood is oozing down its sides.

34 Flagstaff Tower

A safe haven

The simians nonchalantly sprawl on walls, hang in trees, and squat in the middle of the road. The Flagstaff Tower is their preferred perch. The green benches that surround the tower are their favourite seats in the house.

The circular castellated tower in the thickly wooded area of Kamala Nehru Ridge was built in 1828 as a lookout point. It is a relic of the turbulent opposition that the East India Company constantly faced in British India. The tower was probably just a British cantonment structure, built following company protocol, but during the 1857 Uprising, it took on a role it hadn't bargained for.

When Indian sepoys from Meerut rebelled against the British and broke into revolt, they marched towards Delhi. Persuading the reluctant Bahadur Shah Zafar to be their leader, the sepoys swept across the city in a tide of nationalistic fervour. The scared English fled and many – mostly women and children – took refuge in this structure on the evening of May 11 (a few newspapers cruelly mocked the action as "the gathering at Flagstaff Tower"). The English waited in the tower for help to arrive from Meerut, and upon realising it was not forthcoming, fled to Karnal, Punjab. The violence and bloodshed that spread throughout the country resulted in the dissolution of the East India Company and the establishment of the British Raj.

Today, the tower is locked but can still be admired from the outside. At the entrance, vendors selling cold drinks, *bhel* (street food), and chips packets lend a picnicky air to the place.

Only a few tourists and couples seeking privacy visit the ridge, with its noisy parakeets and innumerable birds. It's become a memorial for descendants of the fallen British officers and men. Its dark history seems imagined when contrasted with the sight of a lone runner training for a marathon. For now, it is under a peaceful siege of a monkey army.

Address Kamla Nehru Ridge, Civil Lines | Getting there Vishwavidyalaya Metro Station (Yellow Line) | Hours Daily, sunrise to sunset | Tip There are several interesting locations related to the 1857 Uprising in the Kamla Nehru Ridge area, such as the Khooni Jheel (Bloody Lake). Various stories of paranormal incidents are associated with the place. But if you hear loud laughter, don't panic – it's just the local laughter club (a group that meets to laugh out loud in order to relieve stress) going about its routine.

35__Gadodia Market
The centre of Asia's spice trade

Adjacent to the Fatehpuri Masjid, near Chandni Chowk, a large, arched doorway opens up into a building filled with spice shops and stocking stations. The air is heavy with spicy aromas, and friendly traders on the first floor offer tea or shout out tips on how to control the stinging, burning, and sneezing. This is the Gadodia Market – a large three-story structure in the old *haveli* style, with an open courtyard in the middle.

Built in the 1920s by Seth Lakshmi Narayan Gadodia, this spice trading post offers the best vantage points from which to observe Asia's largest spice market. A climb up the grimy, *paan*-stained stairway, dodging porters carrying sacks full of spices (they have the right of way), leads to a sprawling terrace. A vista straight out of *The Arabian Nights* greets you.

An unceasing buzz – of porters, handcart pullers, and traders – fills the streets below. The market is a cornucopia filled with almonds from California, sultanas from Afghanistan, walnuts from Kashmir, all colours of rock salt, sun-dried mulberries, fragrant rice bags, and mysterious, exotic herbs. The old systems of numbering sacks and loading them on hand-pulled carts remain the same, and the shops from the age of Shah Jahan are still known only by their serial numbers.

The Gadodia market also functions as communal living quarters for migrant spice workers. The aging windows offer glimpses into the lives of these residents. On the terraces of more recent buildings in the centre of the courtyard, you can see workers wash, cook, and wind down after a back-breaking day of work. Young boys walk with familiarity to their spot on the main rooftop for a view that money could never buy. In the distance, the majestic Red Fort stands tall above the chaos of the lanes of Chandni Chowk, while the sight of the peaceful courtyard of the Fatehpuri Masjid next door calms the spice-infused delirium in the alleyways below.

Address Khari Baoli, Chandni Chowk | **Getting there** Chandni Chowk Metro Station (Yellow Line) | **Hours** Mon–Sat 11.30am–7pm | **Tip** Welcome to the Candy Shop. Batashe Wali Gali is just what you need after the intense sensory overload of the Gadodia Market. It is a small lane selling *batashe* (brittle sugar drops), *petha* (pumpkin candy), and *khand* (a type of raw sugar).

36__Garhi Artists Studios

An artists' residence in a hunting lodge

When the government offered the Mughal-era hunting lodge to eminent sculptor Sankho Chaudhuri as a studio, he thought it was a little too large. He handed it over to the Lalit Kala Akademi so that it could be converted into an artists' commune. That's how Delhi's first official artists' residency, Garhi Studios, came into being, in 1976. Sankho Chaudhuri's vision soon became a boon for artists from all over the country.

Today, Delhi is known as the country's art capital, but it wasn't always ahead of the curve. The cities respected for artistic pursuits were the intellectual Kolkata and the innovative Bombay. Garhi Studios became the centre of an artistic renaissance that would transform Delhi's art scene. This 4.2-acre complex provides working space to painters, ceramicists, graphic artists, sculptors, and printmakers. The picturesque village square, now a heritage area, is the pulse of the complex. It is traditional for an artist to leave behind a piece of their work when they depart Garhi Studios. The walkways are flanked by sculptures and artworks created by these former residents.

An idyllic village in the past, the impact of urbanisation is evident here too. Traditional homes are fast being replaced by modern apartments.

In 2014, the studio found itself in the news, as many artists who were there for more than the allowed three years were asked to vacate the premises. With space and essential equipment available to the artists in residence, one can see why some tend to linger. Despite the controversy, the atmosphere of creation in the midst of a rural landscape remains soul nurturing. On cold winter days, artists and villagers are seen basking in the winter sun on the lawns.

The Garhi Studios are now being reinvented, with plans afoot for attracting disadvantaged artists and a programme opening the space to visitors once a month.

Address Kala Kutir, Kalka Garhi Village, Kalka Devi Marg, near East of Kailash | Getting there Kailash Colony Metro Station (Violet Line) | Hours Mon–Fri 10am–6pm | Tip Look for announcements of exhibitions, symposiums, seminars, and workshop events at the Lalit Kala Akademi.

37__Ghazipur Phool Mandi
A riot of flowers

The walking human garlands at Ghazipur Phool Mandi are the first to catch your eye. There's nothing macabre about it, just enterprising flower sellers who drape themselves with marigold strings. This *phool mandi* (flower market), now off the Anand Vihar main road, is an amalgamation of three ancient markets.

The government shifted the main wholesale flower markets from Mehrauli, Connaught Place, and Fatehpuri to Ghazipur. The new destination was envisioned as an ultra-modern market. This, in a way, has changed the fabric of the city. Every flower market in Delhi offered a particular specialty: the Mehrauli market revelled in cut flowers, Fatehpuri was famous for loose marigolds, and Connaught Place was known for its exotic blooms. Stubborn mini *mandis* (markets) have naturally started appearing at Connaught Place and near Qutb Minar.

At the new venue, cut, loose, and exotic flowers are processed in time slots through the day and most of the night. The market is aglow with the brilliance of ornamental flowers from around the world, alongside dependable chrysanthemums and marigolds. Brilliant heliconias compete with glorious birds-of-paradise. Proteas from South Africa, orchids from Sikkim, roses from Nashik and Kullu, and various exotic varieties wrapped in corrugated cardboard vie for your attention from burlap sacks and plastic buckets.

The *chaiwallah* (tea seller), with his tea dispenser perched on a bicycle, adds the aroma of a fresh brew to the heady mix of floral scents, including jasmine, *rajnigandha* (tuberose), and rose petals. Among the *gathris* (bundles) and *gucche* (bunches), women weave garlands with flowers that are heaped at their feet.

Order a cup of tea, and get swept up in the whirlwind of bargaining and conversations. Mornings that begin here only lead to fragrant days.

Address Ghazipur Phool Mandi, Ghazipur | **Getting there** Anand Vihar Metro Station (Yellow Line) | **Hours** Open all day (suggested hours: 4am–9am) | **Tip** As the day wears on, the price of flowers drops. In any case, flowers at Ghazipur are a tenth of the market price. Don't let the morning hours dull your bargaining skills.

38__Ghaziuddin's Madrasa
Asia's oldest educational institution

The *mushairas* (poetry recitals) at Ghaziuddin Madrasa, now known as the Anglo Arabic School, were legendary. Founded by Ghaziuddin Khan, an influential minister and general in Aurangzeb's court, in 1692, the school is older than Old Delhi. Its scalloped arches, covered Persian balconies, wooden doors, and *jharokhas* (small, enclosed three-bayed balconies that jut out like bay windows), bear witness to the Delhi of the Rajputs, Mughals, and British, and of the political turmoil of Independent India.

The sounds of rickety rickshaws, insistent horns, and constant trundling traffic surround the heritage building. The two-story school is one of the few remaining examples of *madrasa* architecture. Ghaziuddin's red Kota sandstone vision has shape-shifted countless times. His tomb, in a latticed screen enclosure near a three-domed mosque, lies next to the dargah of Hazrat Hafiz Sadullah. A few others keep him company.

The British rechristened Ghaziuddin's Madrasa as the Anglo Arabic School and introduced Western subjects like English, mathematics, and natural sciences in 1824. The Vernacular Translation Society was born in 1832 and oversaw many translations of texts into Urdu, becoming a hub of intellectual discourse – so much so that the school was shut down after the 1857 Uprising because the British suspected the involvement of teachers and students in the revolt.

In 1867, it reopened as Anglo Arabic College and was subsequently renamed Delhi College. The Zakir Hussain Delhi College, at Turk-man Gate, where it moved to, still continues the legacy.

Today, the original school's *hujras* (corridors) echo with the typical sounds of student life. The school counts many leading citizens among its alumni, including Pakistan's first prime minister and the founder of Aligarh Muslim University. Delhi's socio-cultural renaissance centre is still going strong.

Address DB Gupta Road, opposite the Ajmeri Gate | **Getting there** New Delhi Metro Station (Yellow Line) | **Hours** Tue & Thu 2pm–3pm. For prior permission, call +91 11 23210863 | **Tip** The Ajmeri Gate is one of the four surviving gateways of Shahjahanabad, or Old Delhi. The gate faces the city of Ajmer, in Rajasthan, hence the name. On the evenings of *mushairas* the gate had to be kept open for the poetically inclined to get home.

39 __ Gulabsingh Johrimal
The emperor's perfumers

Established in 1816, this perfumery in Dariba Kalan is almost two centuries old. Much has changed at this shop since it dabbed scents on the wrists of emperors. Through the march of time, as the elephants of emperors gave way to the horses of the Marathas and camels of the Rajputs, which were in turn were replaced by the trams of Chandni Chowk and the carriages of the British, one thing has remained constant for Gulabsingh Johrimal: its perfumes lure in visitors from around the world. The preparations, some going back centuries, sit in delicately cut crystal *itardans* (perfume bottles) of varying sizes in old rosewood cabinets.

The obsession of the Mughals with *atr* or *ittar*, natural oils and essences, is legendary. In the palaces and *havelis* (mansions) of the rich, scented water from the fountains dispersed luxurious scents in the air, piercing the ennui of summer. This obsession led to the setting up of many perfumeries, which created, blended, and distilled oils.

With each *itardan* uncorked by the shop attendant you are transported from the dusty lanes to exotic mindscapes – by the headiness of the royal rose, the intoxication of jasmine, the sweetness of cedarwood, or the earthiness of *oud* (wood of the tropical Agar tree). There is always a recommendation or a small vial of precious *attar gil* (smell of wet soil) fished out by Mukul Gandhi, one of the sons of veteran perfumer Ram Singh. They themselves are reluctant to name a favourite scent, and the fact that, like most perfumers, they wear no perfume might come as a surprise.

Shoppers exclaim in glee over rare perfumes in delicate bottles embellished with floral designs. Souvenir hunters pick up more practical gifts of handmade soaps and incense. It's almost a circle of life for the scents of Gulab Singh Johrimal, which make their journey from the pastures and fields to a distilling factory, then to the shops, and finally back into thin air.

Address 320, Dariba Kalan, Chandni Chowk, www.gulabsinghjohrimal.com,
info@gulabsinghjohrimal.com, Tel +91 11 23271345 | Getting there Chandni Chowk
Metro Station (Yellow Line) | Hours Daily 11am–9pm | Tip Quench your thirst at the
ancient wells that now function as *piyaons* (watering points) in the lanes of Chandni
Chowk. Ask for directions to the Piyaonwali gali, where an attendant dispenses water from
a small stall to passersby. The cool sweetness is worth waiting for in the small queue.

40__Hanuman Mandir

Red henna and black tattoos

The only time the lane outside Hanuman Mandir was deserted by the *menhdiwallahs* (henna design artists), a constant presence outside the ancient temple, was when Prime Minister Indira Gandhi was assassinated in 1984. The temple (built in 1724 and renovated several times) has been popular with the women of Delhi for bangles, *menhdi* art, and now, tattoos.

Henna artist Shekhar's mother, Sunita, remembers coming here with her mother as a little girl. Today her son accompanies her in decorating the palms of scores of devotees with intricate designs. Tuesday is considered an especially auspicious day, when the temple attracts throngs of people. As Shekhar deftly traces an Arabic pattern with a fish motif at its heart, his mother talks of the mega weddings, engagements, and festivals of which *menhdiwallahs* are an integral part. In India, most auspicious occasions begin with a cool green paste being dribbled onto your hands in patterns that have been passed down for generations and across cultures.

In recent years there has been a peculiar development. The gen-next of the *menhdiwallahs* have morphed into tattoo artists, as is the case with Shekhar. More and more of these tattoo artists are making the lane their home alongside the *menhdi* artists. Tattoos used to be a very rudimentary affair at village fairs, and even at the Hanuman Mandir. The word *Aum* along with an individual's name comprised the basic design. Today, flash-art tattoo designs blend seamlessly with traditional henna patterns, and at times patrons end up opting for a contemporary tattoo design in henna.

The incessant ringing of bells and the smell of henna accompanied by the whir of needles seem the most natural things at Hanuman Mandir. And albums filled with photographs pay homage to the journey traced by this art, from Persia, Afghanistan, Rajasthan, and the hardy villages of the north, all the way to this open-air plaza.

Address Hanuman Mandir, Baba Singh Khark Marg, Connaught Place | **Getting there** Rajiv Chowk Metro Station (Blue/Yellow Line) | **Hours** Daily, evening to late night | **Tip** The subway underpass next to the temple is home to quaint handicraft stores that promote tribal designs and folk art. Keep an eye out for a stall with psychedelic wall art at the far end of the subway.

41__Hardayal Library

Delhi's oldest public library

This library, next to Gandhi Maidan in one of the quieter quarters of Chandni Chowk, has changed names many times during its century-long history. But a library by any name remains redolent and musty-aired with the romance of tomes. It was set up in 1862, as part of the Lawrence Institute, to offer reading material and space to Englishmen and *memsahibs* (wives) of the Raj.

With its graceful arches, a sweeping veranda, large doors, and wooden spiral staircases bathed in natural light, the library is home to around 170,000 books in Hindi, English, Urdu, Arabic, Persian, and Sanskrit (of which 8,000 are rare). A narrow, vertiginous staircase and a few cats have to be navigated to access the more interesting British books that catalogue India's history, flora, fauna, and geographical features. The Rare Collections section holds priceless treasures, including five volumes of *The History of the World*, written by Sir Walter Raleigh and published in 1614, and a 16th-century Persian translation of the *Mahabharata*, by Abu'l-Fazl / Raizi, illuminated in gold. The yellowed crumbling edition of *Relation of Some Yeares Travaile, Begunne Anno 1626*, an account of travels across Asia and Africa by Thomas Herbert, published in 1634, is undoubtedly the most prized of the collection.

For a brief while in 1902, it was named the Delhi Public Library and was shifted to the smaller Kaccha Bagh building. The library's fortune (and its name) took another turn in 1912, when it became the scene for the bomb attack on Lord and Lady Hardinge by freedom fighters led by Lala Hardayal. India's first couple, riding on an elephant, escaped unhurt, but the library bore the brunt. In the bid to pacify his traumatised lordship, the renovated building was named Hardinge Library. Ironically, the library was renamed Hardayal Library post-Independence as a tribute to the very freedom fighter who led the attack.

Address Gandhi Maidan (near the metro station, behind the police station), Chandni Chowk | Getting there Chandni Chowk Metro Station (Yellow Line) | Hours Mon – Sat 10am – 6pm | Tip The *Ghanta Ghar* (Clock Tower), a landmark building that used to be known as the Town Hall (Rai Kedarnath Marg, Town Hall, Chandni Chowk) was the seat of the first Delhi municipality. Today, pigeons seem more besotted with the place than the people who rush by it.

42__Hauz Khas Village
Head to the party town

The ruin of a fort surrounding a placid lake is the most prominent feature of the tiny hamlet called Hauz Khas Village, or HKV. The place dates back to the second city of Delhi, Siri, built by Alauddin Khilji. Hauz Khas was just one ordinary village out of many in this urban landscape until a leading designer opened a store here in the 1980s. Other creative entrepreneurs followed suit and suddenly HKV, a 13th-century settlement, was a cool destination.

In an aggressive city, HKV is a benign hangout where the rules of Delhi drop away. An ancient *madrasa* (educational institution), a mosque, and tombs from both the Tughlaq and Lodi era are now a playground for the city's young and hip. The vertically growing village is a curious amalgam of cafes, independent bookstores, bakeries, restaurants, cartographers, trunk sellers, and tattoo artists. Experimental concepts find a platform for expression here, and the village is a pulsating hub of creativity. In the past, a Creative Arts Village Association initiated programmes that involved the original local residents in this transformation. Past shop owners reminisce about open village nights where discussions over coffee, movies, and art fed the intellectually starved.

Lately, bar crawlers have come to dominate the bohemian vibe. The road to Hauz Khas is jammed almost every evening. It is a dichotomous experience, where bohemia meets suburbia. The early mornings belong to the nature lovers, the lake gazers, and the heritage walkers.

By day, the cafes, quaint shops, and interesting decor shops lure an eclectic crowd. By night, the streets are filled with fedoras, body-con dresses, and dizzyingly high heels. Bawdy club music streams while restaurants' hosts line the lanes, trying to lure in customers with discounts. The puzzling layout of HKV reveals unexpected gems with every visit.

Address Hauz Khas Village, Hauz Khas | Getting there Green Park Metro Station
(Yellow Line) | Tip Deer Park or Bagh-e-Alam just outside the gate of the Hauz Khas
Village is a peaceful place for poetry writing and photography pursuits. It has a small
collection of Mughal-era monuments that lend it a definitive "Delhi edge."

43__Hauz-i-Shamsi
The haunt of a winged horse

At the southern end of Mehrauli is a large reservoir whose waters ripple with the dreams, beliefs, and stories that created it. The walk to this tank requires a leap of faith. It takes you right through the most ancient of the seven cities of Delhi, with its labyrinthine network of lanes and by-lanes, densely packed with shops on either side. Doubts over ever finding it are erased when you round the bend and see the water body appear from among the crowd of residences and bazaar shops.

The *hauz* (water tank), spread over 35,000 square metres, was built in 1230 as a testimony to the grand vision of the slave-dynasty ruler Sultan Iltutmish. Today, it is a pale shadow of its original self. In keeping with the tradition of oral histories, stories about the *hauz* abound. The most intriguing among these is the claim that the sultan had a dream in which the Prophet appears riding a *buraq* (winged horse), telling him to build the water tank. When the ruler visited the place in the morning, he saw the hoofprint of the *buraq*. A domed pavilion, or *chhatri*, in the centre of the *hauz* marks the spot where the hoofprint was seen.

The tranquil environs offer a sharp contrast to the hustle and bustle of the bazaar. During the festival of *Phool Walon ki Sair* (procession of flower sellers), a fair on the banks adds to this buzz. You might even see a believer release a live fish into the waters as an offering for a wish to come true. As the sun rises, a few devotees carry out their circumambulations, sleepy children reluctantly trudge to school, and moorhens and ducks squawk to protest any disturbance in their vicinities. The colour of the surrounding sandstone structures changes with the hour of the day and the waters shimmer in the sunlight. Standing on the footbridge (a later addition) to the pavilion, one can imagine the sultan's boat taking him to the *chhatri* for a reprieve from the sweltering heat.

Address Shamshi Talab, Khandsa Colony, Mehrauli | Getting there Qutb Minar Metro Station (Yellow Line) | Hours Daily, sunrise to sunset | Tip The Jahaz Mahal, built in the shape of a ship, is the palace where the last Mughal emperor, Bahadur Shah Zafar, spent his final days before he was banished to Rangoon, in Burma. It is located at the east end of the Hauz-i-Shamsi complex.

44 Haveli Khazanchi

A secret tunnel for the emperor's treasures

Even in its present decrepit form, this blue *haveli* (mansion) exudes a regal air reminiscent of its glory days. The massive carved wooden doors with scalloped arches wouldn't have been as welcoming of passersby then as they are now. Perhaps sentries stationed at the doors would have brusquely questioned your very presence. Today, you can simply walk in and marvel at its crumbling beauty.

The central courtyard once served as the grand lobby for receiving influential noblemen, and even the emperor. Here, they must have discussed the affairs of the state; and the ground-floor rooms along the courtyard's periphery must have been abuzz with bookkeepers meticulously recording the finances of the empire. After all, this *haveli* was home to the emperor's *khazanchis* (accountants). A rectangular marble pool, now drained, occupies the centre of the courtyard, with beautiful *dalaans* (balconies) overlooking it. An inner courtyard is on a raised platform. Under this platform is the *tekhana* (basement). It is rumoured that a secret underground tunnel that ran from this basement to the Red Fort, serving as a conduit for money, treasures, and accounting journals, was shut down by the government in the 1960s.

The lone descendant of the *khazanchis* who kept the empire's accounts until the reign of the last Mughal emperor, Bahadur Shah Zafar, lives a reclusive life on the ground floor of the *haveli*. Several rooms have been rented out to individuals and families. A young professional who lives here with her cousin's family is effusive about the beauty of the morning hours, when sunlight bathes the marble pillars and lattice screens in golden light. Sadly, this crumbling *haveli* is heading towards the same fate as most others in Shahjahanabad. But with most of its grandeur still intact, it offers a fading chance for us to peek into a past that will soon be lost to history.

Address Haveli Khazanchi, Gali Khazanchi, Chandni Chowk | Getting there Chandni Chowk Metro Station (Yellow Line) | Hours Daily, sunrise to sunset; or at the discretion of the owner | Tip The glorious Red Fort, omnipresent in the distance, is the perfect vantage point from which to survey Shahjahanabad.

45_Heritage Transport Museum

India's first transport museum

Delhi's love for cars is legendary. The broad avenues of the city are made for driving, and most Delhiites believe that a car is a necessity, not a luxury. It seems just perfect then, that the Heritage Transport Museum would find a home in the far-flung Taoru, 75 minutes by car from Delhi and an hour from Gurgaon. It is just one smooth drive away, after all.

A transport wonderland, this anti-museum is a collection of all things wheeled, winged, and motored. Tracing the history of transport in India, it showcases carriage lamps, carbide lamps, and palanquin finials from the days when humans lifted palanquins and yoked horses, camels, bullocks, and even goats to handmade carts. The sight of a restored railway saloon from the 1930s in the train section will make you want to travel back in time. Don't be fooled by the train tickets, posters, and maps though, because this train will only leave the platform in your imagination.

The roads of India come alive in the bus depot section; and the aviation exhibit plays host to a cheery yellow 1940s Piper JC3 cub aircraft suspended mid-air. Expect to be surprised by vintage children's toys like pedal cars and pedi-cycles. There are sections showcasing two-wheelers and even boat models.

The four levels also have a dedicated space for thematic shows. The library is home to books that document the evolution, art, technology, and design of transportation in India. A film about the history of transport is a must-watch. This is the only place to see the *phat-phat* – a half-motorcyle, half-rickshaw contraption pulled by a classic motorcycle like the Triumph or the Enfield, once a popular transport option in Delhi. And for motorheads who wait the entire year for the annual vintage-car rallies, this is a good place to see them up close.

Address Bilaspur, Taoru Road (Major District Road 132), Taoru, Gurgaon (Haryana), www.heritagetransportmuseum.org, info@heritagetransportmuseum.org, Tel +91 11 23718100 | Getting there By Car: Off NH 8 (Bilaspur Chowk) | Hours Tue–Sun 10am–7pm; entrance fee: Rs 300 for adults, Rs 150 for children | Tip If you are interested in the conservation and preservation of vintage beauties, get on the mailing list for regular workshops at the museum.

46__Hijron ka Khanqah
A spiritual retreat for kinnars

The crowded Mehrauli Market, off the main road, is lined with shops of tinsel jewellery, clothes, kitchen essentials, and cheap electronics. In the huddle of stores, you will find no markers showing directions to this 15th-century courtyard with several graves of *kinnars* (transgender people). A low-arched entrance leads to a short flight of stairs that opens on to several tombs laid in perfect symmetry beneath the shade of a giant tree. This is a place venerated by eunuchs across the country. Solemn occasions are marked with visiting the *khanqah* (spiritual centre).

The beautifully maintained *khanqah* is believed to be owned by the eunuchs of Turkman Gate and is one of the oldest graveyards in Delhi. The secretiveness of *kinnars* or *hijras* (an impolite term) extends to all aspects of their lives. So, this little-known graveyard of eunuchs, considered sacred, is shrouded in the same intrigue. Some believe that those buried here have special powers, while others say that only the eunuchs who travelled to Mecca are laid to rest here.

Ancient texts record many *khwajasaras* (eunuchs) playing pivotal roles in the harems, armies, and courts of both Mughal and Hindu rulers. They were conferred with great positions and bequeathed with titles. The chief tomb belongs to one such powerful *kinnar* known as Miyan Saheb, who is believed to have been close to the Sufi saint Qutubuddin Bakhtiar, who lovingly referred to her as *Aapa* (sister). A well-known member of this community was Malik Kafur, who rose through the ranks to become a general in the army of Alauddin Khilji in the late 13th century.

Kinnars from across the country visit the whitewashed courtyard and pay their respects at the tombs of their ancestors. As you watch a group of *kinnars* pray, cook biryani, sing, and dance in this little oasis, you realise that this is their space – a counterpoint to the unequal world outside.

Address Ward 6, (Chatta Wali Gali) Mehrauli | Getting there Qutb Minar Metro Station (Yellow Line) | Hours Daily, sunrise to sunset, depending on the caretaker's presence | Tip Madhi Masjid, with its dainty ornamentation, Rajasthani *jharokhas* (latticed balconies), and fortified walls with turrets, is very close to the Jain Dadabadi Temple.

47 India Gate

The tale of an empty canopy

A large arc designed by Edward Lutyens frames the central axis of Rajpath, formerly called Kingsway. With a height of 42 feet, it inspires a patriotic fervour that soars much higher than that. Even taller at 72 feet, right across the India Gate is an empty sandstone cupola that seems bereft of any purpose. Few know that until the 1960s, a 50-foot-tall imperious George V statue stood under the canopy.

The forlorn sculpture of George V now stands at Coronation Park (see p. 40), where several British statues removed from various locations in Delhi have been installed. The statue, by Charles Sargeant Jagger, was commissioned on the occasion of the coronation of the king for the last *durbar* (gathering). The monument was "a gift of the Maharaja of Kapurthala and a few unspecified princes," writes author Mary Ann Steggles in her book, *Statues of the Raj*. The coronation robes, etched in marble, fall as softly as any fabric might, covering the plinth on which the statue now stands. Wearing the Imperial State Crown and holding the British globus cruciger and sceptre – its stately veneer now damaged – the figure faces the Coronation pillar in this expansive park in North Delhi instead of the grand Kingsway.

In 1981, a question was posed in the parliament regarding the deserted canopy. It was suggested that a statue of Mahatma Gandhi should occupy this place of honour. Ram Vanji Sutar, a respected sculptor, was tasked with creating a statue. He is well known for his Gandhi busts, which adorn pedestals in countries around the world. Yet his two models, one of Gandhi sitting in a meditating pose, and the other of Gandhi leading a march against British rule, still await a green light.

Perhaps the poetic empty canopy says a lot more than any statue could. Lit up in the evenings, just like the India Gate, the empty space makes an eloquent statement.

Address Rajpath, India Gate | **Getting there** Central Secretariat Metro Station (Violet / Yellow Line) / Udyog Bhawan Metro Station (Yellow Line) | **Tip** The Boat Club on Rajpath is a great picnic spot for families, and has recently revived boating, which offers the opportunity to see the historic surroundings from a new perspective (boating hours: 2pm – 9pm).

48 Indira Gandhi National Centre of Arts

A grove, in memoriam

The guard seated in the shade of the glorious mango tree at the National Centre of Arts might think you have lost your way and guide you toward the usual exhibition areas. If you share your reasons for being there, he probably won't know what you are talking about and offer you directions to the media centre. Pretend to heed his advice, but keep walking past the government bungalow-style office he points at. Behind it, there is a small pond with a stone slab protruding from its middle, surrounded by a modest grove of five trees.

It looks ordinary but holds great cultural significance. These five trees are the most important native trees of India. The *Asvattha*, better known as the Bodhi tree, is a symbol of enlightenment. The *Nyagrodha*, a large tree with roots that grow branches and branches that grow roots again, is a metaphor for the metaphysical cycle of life. The *Asoka* tree, mentioned in classical and medieval Indian culture and art, represents fertility, while the *Arjuna* tree is supposed to be the receptacle of purity and clarity. And the *Kadamba* is a celebration of life itself.

The late Prime Minister Rajiv Gandhi established this centre in 1985 in memory of his mother, Indira Gandhi. He planted this grove as part of the institution's inaugural ceremony. The five trees are symbolic of the various art departments of the centre dedicated to the preservation of the arts and cultural experiences in the country.

The significance of these trees is lost in time and very few visitors even know of the grove. But in an era where the predominant method of immortalising public figures is to commission gaudy statues and grandiose installations, there's something distinctly poignant about a leader's legacy and a nation's ancient natural beliefs being commemorated together through a living grove.

Address 11, Man Singh Road, www.ignca.gov.in, Tel +91 11 23388155 | Getting there Central Secretariat Metro Station (Gate No. 2, Violet Line) | Hours Mon–Sat 9.30am–5pm | Tip Extending the idea of nature being the source of creation, five rocks from the five major rivers – Sindhu, Ganga, Kaveri, Mahanadi, and the Narmada – are also installed in sculptural form within the same premises.

49__Iroha Bakery
Taste of Tokyo in Gurgaon

A quaint Japanese bakery right in the thick of a bustling shopping centre in Gurgaon is this neighbourhood's sweetest secret. After losing your way and circling the market a few times, the process of finding this little bakery just adds to the appeal of Iroha. It is uncannily like being lost in a Tokyo shopping district, where discovering hidden bars and quirky joints is part of the experience.

Nestled among grocers, tailors, and cheap electronic vendors, Iroha mostly caters to a Japanese expat community, offering a mix of breads, cookies, desserts, and savouries in a Zen-like compact setting. A display counter where every patron lingers over the day's sweet temptations occupies most of the space. The cosy low-level seating in one corner is barely enough to fit two people.

True to its name, Iroha (the "basics" in Japanese) is Gurgaon's introduction to the ABCs of Japanese desserts. Subtly flavoured confections are integral to the elaborate Japanese tea tradition. Unlike the Western concept of a post-meal dessert, the Japanese custom is to indulge in mildly sweet treats that take the edge off the bitter taste of tea. Toward evening, a stream of Japanese matrons, businessmen, and occasional Indian patrons make a beeline to Iroha. Most days, they find that their favourite pastries have already flown off the shelves as the bakery provides a very limited and seasonal menu.

At Iroha, delectable *choux* pastry filled with cream or custard, crisp madeleines, subtle *matcha*-flavoured teacakes, financiers, jellies, and cookies share shelves with traditional Japanese sweets, like *shiratama zenzai (*sweet red beans with *mocha* or Japanese rice-cake pillows with *mocha*) and simple *mochi* (Japanese chocolate). If you're planning to visit during the cherry-blossom season, make sure that you get to the bakery in time for the rare sakura sweets, chef Sakae Omori's finest creations.

Address 144–146, Ground Floor, Vyapar Kendra, Phase I, Sushant Lok, Gurgaon, www.iroha-india.com, Tel +91 124 4147401 | **Getting there** HUDA City Centre Metro Station (Yellow Line) | **Hours** Tue–Sun 11am–7pm | **Tip** A short walk away, the Galleria shopping complex (DLF Phase IV, Sector 28), with a sort of Italian town-square feel, is a delightful open-air space with a large fountain in the centre surrounded by high-end boutiques and coffee shops.

50__Isa Khan's Tomb

India's oldest sunken garden

The sidekick, no matter how talented, never gets to be the star of the show. However, every once in a while, he triumphs over his starry counterpart and gets his moment in the spotlight. In this case, the star is one of Delhi's most iconic monuments, Humayun's Tomb, and the sidekick happens to be the older tomb of Isa Khan Niyazi, a nobleman in the court of Sher Shah Suri, the Afghan ruler who defeated Humayun.

Situated near the entrance of the complex, just to the right, Isa Khan's Tomb is usually missing from rushed Delhi itineraries. However, wayward visitors who chance upon it are rewarded with a unique sight: a remarkable octagonal tomb set in a sunken garden. It takes a while to realise that this tomb is different because it is positioned at eye level, unlike the Mughal monuments that demand craning the neck.

Spreading out at your feet, the sunken garden, neither magnificent nor ostentatious, is a simple, tranquil patch of green that circles the tomb and follows it up the stairway. Unearthed during the recent restoration efforts of the Archaeological Survey of India (ASI) and the Aga Khan Trust, this was an important discovery. It took the removal of more than 3,000 cubic metres of earth to reveal the true nature of this garden. And with its unearthing came significant cultural knowledge of landscaping, lifestyle, and the architectural designs of the Afghan invaders, distinguishing this garden from the ones that were built by the Mughals.

Central Asian conquerors of India were all known to be united in their love of gardens. Closely symbolic of paradise, the garden served as a nostalgic reminder of their native homes. Centuries later, gardens continue to lend a quiet grandeur and a regal charm to the capital. After all, even the fierce Babur felt that gardens tamed "… that charmless and disorderly Hind."

Address Mathura Road, Humayun's Tomb complex | Getting there Central Secretariat Metro Station (Yellow Line) | Hours Daily, sunrise to sunset. Entrance fee for foreign tourists: Rs 250. | Tip The elusive concept of world peace and brotherhood finds expression at the Vishwa Shanti Stupa within the Millennium Indraprastha Park (Sarai Kale Khan, 7am–7pm). The beautiful statues of Buddha and a series of stone sculptures at the Peace Pagoda will definitely intrigue you.

51__Ishq-e-Dilli
India's first mapped architectural projection show

The fading light of the sun usually sees people emptying the streets of the city. In contrast, at the Purana Qila, people trickle into the massive red sandstone-and-marble doorway, and walk towards the crumbling ruins of the Old Fort. The attraction is the country's first permanent projected art installation. As dusk sets in, the audience settles, the lights dim, and strains of Aamir Khusro's composition *Chaap Tilak*, accompanied by visuals of *kathak* (a dance form), fill the air.

The tale of cities within cities begins with the defeat of Rajput ruler Prithviraj. A whirl of graphics and colours brings larger-than-life characters from history books alive. The dust of history becomes glitter and settles on the ruins, as tales of wars, murders, spiritualism, and intrigue unfold. Delhi, the temptress, seduces emperors who wage wars, who win, lose, rise, and fall, even as the city goes through ten incarnations. The captivating show traces the history from Qila Rai Pithora to Qutb-Mehrauli, Kilokri, and the city of Siri from the Khilji dynasty, through Tughlaqabad, Jahanpanah, Firozabad, Shahjahanabad, Lutyens' Delhi, and finally to modern-day New Delhi.

The pace of the *son-et-lumiere* is relentless and the number of events immense, but it is packaged in an engaging, entertaining narrative with a running time of slightly over an hour. Technology buffs will find themselves walking to the projection booth afterwards to chat up Manish Kumar, who has been operating the show since 2011.

The L-shaped monument lends itself beautifully to the intriguing layers of the city's past. The Humayun Darwaza gateway with its numerous chambers and crumbling cupolas provides depth to the stories. The glint of swords, the swirling costumes, and the kohl-rimmed eyes seem to follow you long after you have exited the fort. Delhi will never be the same for you after watching this spectacle.

Address Purana Qila, Mathura Road | **Getting there** Pragati Maidan Metro Station (Blue Line) | **Hours** Sep–Oct, daily 7pm–8pm (Hindi), 8.30pm–9.30pm (English); Nov–Jan, daily 6pm–7pm (Hindi), 7.30pm–8.30 pm (English); Feb–Apr, daily 7pm–8pm (Hindi), 8.30pm–9.30 pm (English); May–Aug, daily 7.30pm–8.30 pm (Hindi), 9pm–10pm (English). Entrance fee: Rs 80 for adults, Rs 40 for children. | **Tip** You will see Humayun trip and fall to his death in the show. His library, Sher Mandal, where this happened, is inside the same Old Fort. It was built by Humayun's arch nemesis, Sher Shah Suri, but was converted by Humayun into his library, making the accident somehow more ominous.

52 — Jahanara Begum's Tomb
The Empress of Princesses

The walk to the *dargah* (shrine) of the Sufi saint Hazrat Nizamuddin Auliya is an assault of smells, sounds, and sights. A lane, thick with incense smoke and a cacophony of voices, brings you to the centre of a courtyard that throbs with energy. In one corner, facing the tomb of the Sufi saint, next to a domineering mosque, is the humble tomb of a forgotten princess, Jahanara (1614–1681), the eldest daughter of Mughal emperor Shah Jahan.

Behind cobwebbed lattice screens, the tomb is open to the sky. The Persian inscription at the head of her tomb reads, "He is the Living, the Sustaining. Let no one cover my grave except with greenery, for this very grass suffices as a tomb cover for the poor. The annihilated *fakeera* Lady Jahanara, Disciple of the lords of Chishti, Daughter of Shah Jahan the Warrior (may God illuminate his proof)."

In contrast to the neighbouring tombs of the Sufi saint and poet Amir Khusro, which are adorned in flowers, covered by *chadars*, and fanned by *pankahs*, Jahanara's tomb is bare and undisturbed. Its marble edges serve as support for women who have their eyes focused on Auliya's shrine. They are not allowed to enter the shrine, a discrimination Auliya would surely have objected to.

Jahanara enjoyed an exalted position in the court of both her father Shah Jahan and brother Aurangzeb. Her wisdom was unquestioned, and the freedoms she enjoyed were far above those typically afforded to women in her time. That she had several lovers, and on most nights sang, danced, and drank till she passed out, just adds to the intrigue of Jahanara.

Her quest for spirituality and her humanity is well recorded in the books she wrote, the poems she composed, and the architectural works she commissioned. While Jahanara's tomb remains nondescript, her legacy endures in the form of Chandni Chowk, Delhi's oldest and most vibrant market.

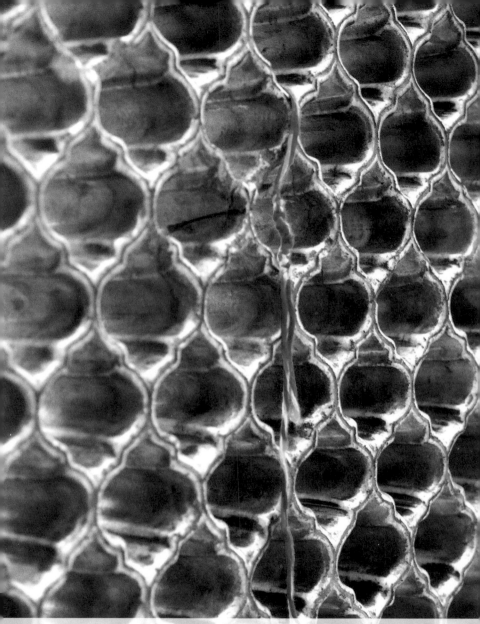

Address Dargah Nizammudin Auliya, Old Nizamuddin Bazaar, www.nizamuddinaulia.org |
Getting there JLN Stadium Metro Station (Violet Line) | **Hours** Daily 5am – 10pm.
Thursdays are the designated days of worship at the *dargah*. Men and women need to cover
their heads and women are not allowed to enter shrine chambers. | **Tip** The *qawwali* (Sufi
music) session in honour of the Sufi saint weaves a trance as the crowd, the pickpockets, and
the constant hustling falls away. The *qawwals* start at approximately 5.30pm and 9pm every
evening, earlier in winter.

53__Jain Studio
Hand-painted custom Bollywood art

The muezzin's call makes a soothing setting to tired cycle-rickshaw drivers catching a few winks in a lane opposite the Ghata Masjid. Nearby, in a rundown garage, large canvases surround artist Vijay Singh, as his broad strokes bring to life a scene from a Bollywood blockbuster. Except the main characters in the poster are not film stars, but Singh's clients who have commissioned the piece. Since hand-painted film posters have been long abandoned by the film industry in favour of digital posters, the open-air Jain Studio is a welcome anomaly.

In the 1970s, Jain Studio created hand-painted Bollywood posters announcing Dilip Kumar's melodramas, Hema Malini's potboilers, and Dharmendra's action films. Vijay Singh, then an errant youngster, reluctantly gave up his hobbies of kite flying and *kabutarbazi* (pigeon handling) at the insistence of his brother Ranjeet, for an apprenticeship under painter Keshu Rai. However, with the arrival of vinyl, this studio came to a standstill.

Years later, a Frenchman got Vijay to do a few personalised posters. Word spread and work started trickling in. New Yorkers Dave and Jenny Prager tracked him down to create a poster for a Christmas card. It ended up as the cover for Dave's book *Deliriously Delhi*, recounting the couple's Delhi adventures.

Vijay's distinctive art draws a different clientele now. Embassy staff, travellers, local businessmen, collectors, and corporates find their way to the studio. Every poster is unique. Each one showcases a theme and is some odd iteration of an already-popular commercial movie poster. The client could play an angry villain, a nubile heroine, or a swashbuckling hero. Details like the appropriate expressions, archetypal bright pigments, and distinctive costumes are critical. This is a labour of love for an artist who is among the last custodians of a dying art form.

Address By-lane near the Daryaganj fire station, 6/6 Darya Ganj, near Ghata Masjid. If you can speak Hindi, call Vijay on +91 9268144532; otherwise, you can speak to Ranjeet, his brother, at +91 9999629382, ranjeet_2870@rediffmail.com | **Getting there** New Delhi Metro Station (Yellow Line) | **Hours** By appointment | **Tip** A lush park surrounds Gandhi's final resting place, Raj Ghat, east of Daryaganj, where an eternal flame burns in memory of his contribution to the nation and mankind. The memorials of some of the most significant political leaders of India surround Raj Ghat (open sunrise to sunset).

54__Jantar Mantar
The lane of protests

A visit to Jantar Mantar in Jaipur is usually made to marvel at the world's largest sundial, which was built entirely of stone by the Maharaja Jai Singh II during the 1720s. But at the Jantar Mantar in Delhi, it is often the scene outside the gates that draws more attention.

A maelstrom of political demonstrations makes this lane an odd blend of tourists and protestors. Before politicians hijacked it to hold their rallies, the Boat Club lawns near Rajpath used to double as a space for ordinary citizens to stage protests. Jantar Mantar has since been adopted by activists across the nation as an unofficial venue in which to gather and register their dissent.

It was here that the veteran leader Anna Hazare gave the clarion call for a movement against corruption in 2011. Since then, the road at Jantar Mantar has been seeing protestors of different hues almost on a daily basis. Entire villages travel to the city to bring attention to crippling issues like drought, debt, and government apathy. There is always an air that something is about to go down. On-site television crews wait in anticipation to capture any sensational byte. Newspaper reporters and photographers can be seen mingling with the demonstrators, looking for a story. A group of tough-looking policemen are always on standby.

Outside the observatory, huge vats of food simmer to feed the army of demonstrators. A mini industry has come up to provide snacks, Nehru jackets, and sunglasses. The colourful, traditionally-garbed activists in the heart of the city create quite a stir. Recently, the government ordered that protests here be restricted to a window from 9am to 4pm after a farmer hanged himself from a tree in protest. Demonstrators who usually camped out at Jantar Mantar had to find another place to rest. The street is the pulse of conflicts simmering across India's rural and urban landscapes.

Address Sansad Marg, Jantar Mantar | **Getting there** Janpath Metro Station (Violet Line) | **Tip** Janpath or People's Path, formerly the Queen's Way, is a vibrant shopping street selling mostly Indian handicraft items, clothes, and footwear. A round library-*cum*-bookstore is a favourite stop for the city's book lovers.

55 Jhandewalan Hanuman Statue

Delhi metro's poster boy

How do you take a photograph of a 108-foot-tall orange statue? The Jhandewalan Hanuman Statue looks kindly upon its visitors as they experiment with innovative angles for that perfect shot. No stranger to attention, the famous monkey-deity is now among the most iconic landmarks in Delhi, symbolic of modernity co-existing with the city's long chequered history. It's even featured in Ishq-e Dilli (see p. 110), the light and sound show aimed at introducing travellers to the tale of Delhi's many cities.

For many who take the Blue Line to Dwarka, the blur of a peculiar orange is a regular sight while passing the Karol Bagh metro station. Erected in 1997, it has changed the skyline of west Delhi. The 1930s-era Sankat Mochan temple is relatively new when compared to Delhi's ancient past. A plaque states that the origin of the statue lies within the hazy dreamscape of the temple priest. The deity appeared in founder Mahant Nagababa Sevagirji Maharaj's dream and expressed a wish for a statue to be erected on this site.

Today, the brightly painted statue towers over the temple, with the heads of vanquished evil spirits at its feet. The temple entrance is shaped like the wide-open fanged mouth of a demon. The idea that this wards off bad luck is therapeutic for believers. Not surprisingly, the temple has many visitors paying obeisance, hoping for the divine grace to shine on them.

Inside, the chambers are bathed in incense, floral offerings, and unfettered faith. The highlight, though, is when the statue showcases Hanuman's devotion to Lord Ram and Sita. On one day a week, enabled by electronics, the statue tears open its chest to reveal statues of them inside. Technology and faith converge in this retelling of a legend, yet again reinforcing Delhi's forever-evolving identity.

Address Jhandewalan Extension, Karol Bagh | Getting there Jhandewalan Metro Station (Blue Line) | Hours Daily 5am–10pm. Mechanical show, Tue 8.15am & 8.15pm | Tip The nearby Bhuli Bhatiyari ki Mahal in the Central Ridge Reserve Forest is a 14th-century hunting lodge built during the rule of Feroz Shah Tughlaq. The palace in the park is very popular, and on the haunted trail list for those seeking paranormal thrills.

56_Khoj Studios
An alternative space for artists

The clean lines of exposed brick at Khoj Studios make you wish that bricks would never be subjected to the ignominy of plaster again. Its broken-tiled courtyard is a refined metaphor for the fractured contemporary art scene in the country. The three floors of Khoj are home to talented artists from throughout India who are busy creating works that most large galleries would not dare to feature. Five studio spaces, guest houses, a kitchenette, a library, lounge space, a media lab, a cafe, meeting rooms, and a terrace that hosts gatherings form this artists' paradise.

"Expect the unexpected" is a cliché, but the events that happen within the confines of this meditative and creative space are exactly that. From experimental film screenings to food presented in the context of art, to the playful use of sound in conceptual installations, the multidisciplinary artistic creations on display are designed to challenge the senses and open minds. Khoj's initiatives to engage the local community in its activities, like giving makeovers to local shops and making clay toys with children from the neighbourhood, contribute to the enclave's unique artistic aura.

Finding your way to Khoj near Press Enclave Road is a study in contrasts. Khirki, an urban village with unpaved streets located not far from the buzz of malls and chain restaurants, seems an unlikely home for this hip artists' residency program that acts as an incubator for unconventional ideas. International artists thrive on the exchange of ideas and dialogue that Khoj fosters with several programmes.

The Khoj International Artists' Association was set up in 1997 in defiance of the lack of networks, collaborative support, and spaces for contemporary artists here. Over the years, the organisation has evolved into an amphitheatre for the senses and a sanctuary for artistic experimentation that pushes the envelope.

Address S-17, Khirki Extension, www.khojworkshop.org, Tel +91 11 65655873 | Getting there Malviya Nagar Metro Station (Yellow Line) | Hours Cafe: Mon–Sat 10am–7pm; check for event times online | Tip A five-minute walk via the Khirki Main Road will take you to the mosque Khirki Masjid, so named for its windows. It is believed to have been designed for the exclusive use of women.

57__Kumhar Gram
The largest pottery colony in India

On the outskirts of west Delhi, a settlement of artisans is engaged in carrying forward the legacy of the Indus Valley civilisation. The 700-odd potter families living here have been spinning wheels in the city since the 1970s, but their relationship with earth, water, and fire goes back generations, with roots in a village in Rajasthan. Though integral to the cityscape, the demands of an eternally evolving metropolis have seen this community relocated from their earlier central Delhi home to the city limits.

The way to the village is through dusty roads and myriad alleyways. Black spirals from kilns serve as beacons. Rows of earthen *diyas* (lamps) line the courtyards of homes, while flowerpots and *matkis* (pitchers) are stacked in neat rows against walls (that are often themselves made of broken pots). Street sides are dotted with mounds of clay, sourced specially from a district in Haryana, which the women beat with a stick and sieve to prep for moulding. This is an industrious community, and there isn't a hand in the village that isn't engaged or muddied. Some mould or carve patterns while children colour the pots, and still others bake them in mud kilns seen outside every home.

The *Kumhars* or *Prajapatis* (potters) here are celebrated ambassadors of their craft, travelling around the world on artist exchange programs. Many are specialists in niche forms, like life-size figures or fibreglass work.

Shopaholics with a clay fetish can delight at the display of kitchenware, piggy banks, *kulhads* (glasses), wall hangings, foot scrubs, and bird feeders found in almost all the homes here. Visitors can try their hand at the wheel when on a group tour. Half-day tours are an easier way to navigate the village, and are organised by Indomania Tours in collaboration with the NGO South Asia Foundation, which has adopted this potters' colony.

Address Kumhar Gram, Sainik Vihar, Sainik Enclave, Vikaspuri | **Getting there** Janakpuri (West) Metro Station (Blue Line) | **Hours** Daily, sunrise to sunset. For a guided tour, contact Indomania at Tel +91 8860223456 | **Tip** Go home laden with clay utility and art objects wrapped very sensibly in eco-friendly paper, as opposed to plastic bags that are synonymous with Delhi. So come armed with a big cotton bag.

58__Kuremal Mohanlal Kulfiwala

The cool fruit stuffed with ice cream

For *Dilliwallas* who love to drive long distances to get their ice-cream fix, Kuremal Mohanlal Kulfiwala, the hole-in-the-wall *kulfi* (ice cream) shop in Sitaram Bazaar, is a beacon in summers. In the midst of tangled electrical wires, cobwebbed *havelis* (mansions), and dusty streets, the siren call of its metal freezer beckons to hundreds of loyal patrons late into the night.

This famous family establishment sells its brand of *kulfis* to most ice-cream companies, yet keeps the old shop open. The pink and green candy-coloured bare room is as minimal as it can get. It offers patrons a small marble ledge and a few plastic chairs as seating. Keep cool while making a choice from more than 60 flavours, like tamarind, rose, kiwi, *falsa* (local fruit), black jamun, *paan* (betel nut leaf), custard apple, and banana. Dry fruit, natural essences like rose and *kewda*, and seasonal fruits available in the market dictate the flavours, so no trip is ever the same.

The stars of the show are the stuffed-fruit *kulfis*: hollowed fruit filled with a similarly flavoured, impossibly velvety ice cream. Besides the king of mangoes, the Alphonso, there are stuffed pomegranates, oranges, guavas, apples, and even litchis. Select the flavour, and the server meticulously prepares it for you, making neat slices. Sink your teeth through the textures and sensations of creamy *kulfi* and cold fruit.

Pandit Kuremal, the founder, first plied residents with milky cold *kulfi* from a single pushcart in 1908. By the 1970s, the business, then run by his descendants, had multiple pushcarts. The family opened a shop in 1975, and today this little place can claim to serve some of the best *kulfis* in Delhi. In the old city, which is fanatical about its food and has insatiable appetites, Kuremal Mohanlal Kulfiwala is a gastronomic achievement spanning generations.

Address 1165–66, Kucha Pati Ram, Sita Ram Bazaar | Getting there Chawri Bazaar Metro Station (Yellow Line) | Hours Mon–Sat noon–8pm | Tip The Heritage Haveli (1834, Gali Chowk Shah Mubarak, Kucha Pati Ram, Sitaram Bazar, www.heritagehavelidelhi.in), a 150-year-old restored *haveli*, is a good example of both Mughal and colonial influences.

59___Lal Kuan Bazaar
Where kites get their wings

Discussions at Iqra Kite Maker, one of the oldest shops in Lal Kuan Bazaar, are intense. The customer almost always has bandaged fingers, a result of wielding glass-coated *manjha* (threads) that are tied to kites. They bend the kite, weigh it in their hands, and consider whether this is the kite to win all aerial duels.

The sport requires an entire set of skills. At first, you get to be the designated kite launcher. Next come the *charkha*-holding (spindle) duties. You are then given a few minutes of flying time when there is no *pencha* (cutting competition) underway. Learning the nuances of a balanced kite and controlling its movement follows. The honour of actually flying a kite is bestowed on an initiate only once these skills are mastered. Using glass and the paste of sago or rice to coat the thread is another art the initiate needs to learn. An aerodynamically perfect kite requires a balance of art and science that kite flyers never take for granted.

The kite shops of Lal Kuan Bazaar have provided kites in all shapes, colours, and sizes to generations of kite enthusiasts in Delhi. Each family has a favourite kite shop, and invariably, the second and the third generation patronise the same shop for years. The bazaar once used to be full of kite shops. Some of them have started selling utensils, making space for kites only during the kite season.

Still, the whirring of homemade *charkha* machines that spool thread onto the spindles fills the lanes; and the faces of film stars and cricketers beam down from the latest kite designs lining the walls. Squint at the sky during kite season in Old Delhi, and you will see hundreds of them dotting your field of vision. Cries of cheering, whistling, and booing are exchanged across rooftops. Exclamations like *lappet* ("spool it in") and *wo kata* ("it's cut") fill the air. For *Dilliwallahs*, kite-flying is not just another pastime, it's an obsession.

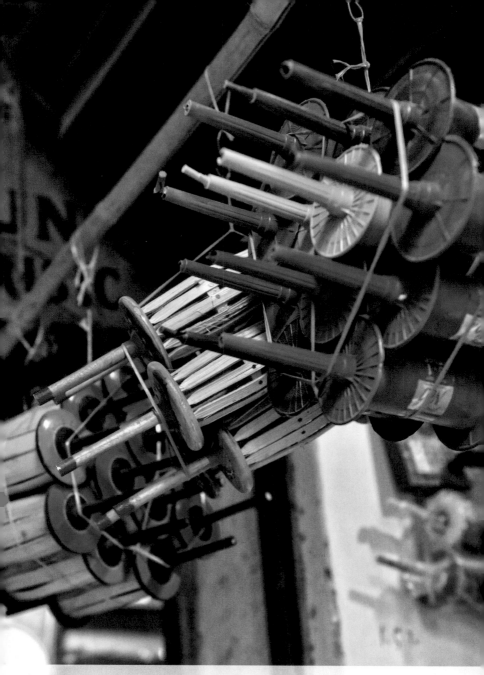

Address Shahjahanabad, Old Delhi | **Getting there** Chawri Bazaar Metro Station (Yellow Line) | **Hours** Daily, sunrise to sunset | **Tip** Sharmaji's spice shop in Lal Kuan is a local institution. His blends are the stuff of legends, and he is also the one-stop shop for Delhi's finest restaurants.

60__The Lanes of Shahpur Jat

An open-air street-art gallery

A turban-wearing man lounges on a *charpoy* (a string bed) with a *hookah* (an oriental tobacco pipe with a long, flexible tube) at his feet. On the wall behind him, a bright graffitied sign reads, "Bond." The scene is bizarre but that is Shahpur Jat for you. Every corner of this urban village offers a visual delight in the form of a breathtaking mural, a gritty graffitied wall, or a surreal piece of street art. The neighbourhood has been taken over by spray-paint and stencil-touting hipsters.

The residents are not complaining, though. Home to leather craftsmen, tailors, and *zardozi karigars* (gold embroidery workmen), the alleyways of Shahpur Jat are accustomed to artistic whims and fancies. A tailoring shop owner is appreciative of a piece of graffiti that declares him a "Master Tailor." Another local woman wishes that, instead of the abstract art on her wall, she had something like the first mural in the area, artist Anpu's *Billi*, which has evolved into a landmark of sorts. While the residents were initially reluctant, now they are eager to offer the artists their walls as canvases.

Artists from around the world gather here through the initiative of the organisation *St+Art*, which encourages street art throughout the country. From delicate artwork on a jewellery store (look for HP Jewellers) by Danish artist Alina Vergnano to Yantr's mechanical creations, and from Daku's smart Hindi script on a garbage bin to the huge bright mural featuring Bollywood star Nargis, by Ranjit Dhaiya, there's a cornucopia of styles on display here.

Walking through the art-filled lanes of Shahpur Jat is like being on a treasure hunt, as you weave your way through a maze of houses, traditional shops, and handcarts. Most shops have a map of the area to help you find your way around, but getting lost is highly recommended. There is always a colourful surprise awaiting you, just around the corner.

Address Shahpur Jat, Siri Fort | Getting there Qutb Minar Metro Station (Yellow Line) | Hours Daily, sunrise to sunset | Tip The Pot Belly, a quaint restaurant straight past Slice of Italy with two entrances – one a normal stairwell and the other a vertigo-inducing spiral – offers a one-of-a-kind menu of Bihari delicacies. Their "Mutton Chhap" is a melt-in-your-mouth plateful of spiced stew.

61__Lawns of Rajpath
The trees of the empire

The leafy avenues of Lutyens' Delhi serve as a distinctive badge that the city wears with pride. While the gardens created by the Mughals were definitely an inspiration and road map for these avenues, the trees chosen by the British for planting along the boulevards reveal a lot about their vision for an imperial Delhi. A century later, the selection continues to raise eyebrows. The British, desirous of evergreen avenues, were adamant: no deciduous trees. The grand vision for their new capital had no place for something as silly as shed leaves.

Pradip Krishen's *Trees of Delhi* dissects this evolution of avenues, making an effort to understand the different species of trees and how the vegetation of Delhi has changed over the years. As nature would have it, every single species native to Delhi is deciduous. So, all of the 13 tree species seen lining these streets are not native to the city (except the *amaltas*). These include *neem* (Indian Lilac), *arjuna*, *peepal* (sacred fig), *baheda* (bastard myrobalan), Buddha myrobalan, and the humble *jamun* (Indian blackberry), which also had to meet the stringent height, shade, life span, and foliage requirements. Most of the research into which botanicals were suitable were carried out at Sunder Nursery (see p. 212).

On the lawns of Rajpath, set among the *jamun* trees, is a place to escape, relax, and catch up with the day's events. The disciplined line of lamp posts alongside the trees offers a Zen horizon. While eavesdropping on conversations (unsurprisingly political), a continuous stream of snacking is mandatory. If reading a book with your back on the lush grass is on your agenda, rest assured, you will be lulled into a nap barely a few pages in. Any resistance is futile, as the serene setting conspires with the swaying trees, forcing you to forget all worldly concerns. Better pack something soft to use as a cushion and yield to the temptation.

Address Near Rajpath, C-Hexagon | **Getting there** Central Secretariat Metro Station (Yellow Line) | **Hours** Daily, sunrise to sunset | **Tip** A five-minute walk down to Man Singh Road, the Shahi Masjid Zabta Ganj is a reminder of the old settlements that gave way to New Delhi. The white mosque, hidden among the trees, is best approached from the wooden bridge.

62 Lodhi Gardens

One man's trash can, another man's canvas

There is an air of sophistication around Lodhi Gardens. Peacocks strut through the wooded expanse in quiet disdain. Perched up in the foliage, squirrels let their disapproval be known to a tourist gliding on a battery-run skateboard. On the steps of Sheesh Gumbad, college students serenade ancient graves. The rose gardens perfume the tombs at Bara Gumbad. A bonsai garden and a greenhouse attract gardening hobbyists. On the jogging tracks of Lodhi Gardens, residents in tracksuits run in dignified silence around Lodhi-era monuments, as if it were the most natural thing in the world to exercise alongside the tombs of emperors.

What doesn't quite fit in this scheme is the presence of quirkily painted trashcans everywhere you turn. These garbage receptacles resemble an artist's canvas. They are covered with sunny visuals, dark brooding visions, dainty twirls, stoic public messages, and even a few aliens. The 150 cans dotting this historic garden are part of a unique art endeavour by Delhi Street Art, an initiative aimed at creating Delhi's largest open-air public art installation. It has the tacit approval of the New Delhi Municipality Corporation (NDMC).

In a society where garbage is considered untouchable at worst and someone else's problem at best, Delhi Street Art founder Yogesh Saini wanted to drastically change people's attitudes towards trash disposal. The project started out by asking professional artists to paint the bins, and has evolved into a collaborative effort where citizens are invited to participate. Since the first invitation went out, several more rounds have been organised and the results are spread throughout the area.

Sikander Lodhi's tomb looms over his little kingdom of picnickers, couples in love, mommies with strollers, and fitness freaks with their apps. This is truly Delhi's happiest place; the garbage bins make it the funkiest, too.

Address Lodhi Gardens, Lodhi Road, Facebook: Delhi Street Art, delhistreetart@gmail.com | Getting there Jor Bagh Metro Station (Yellow Line) | Hours Daily 6am – 7pm | Tip The Lodhi Garden restaurant, adjacent to the park, popular for its Sunday brunches and high tea, provides romantic al fresco dining, perfect for when you haven't packed a picnic basket.

63 Lothian Cemetery

The oldest Christian cemetery in Delhi

Hundreds of tombs dot the landscape of Delhi's many cities. They remain like sentinels of time, standing long after their inhabitants have been forgotten. One such graveyard is the Lothian Cemetery on Lothian Road. The British established it for the city's Christian population in 1808. It is believed that there used to be a Muslim cemetery in this location. With all the unearthing, building, and rebuilding that each conquering army has subjected the city to, it is quite possible. Until some years ago, refugees from the Partition lived alongside the graves.

Down the small lane, the grounds are silent and deserted. Once a well cared for cemetery, it now has small shrubs peeking through cracks in its tombstones. After a century, a few tombs still retain some of the splendour bestowed on them by loved ones. Grieving spots, some with brick and limestone cenotaphs in the shape of a *chattri* (cupola), others with large Celtic crosses, tell stories of remembrance and loss. One tombstone mourns the death of a three-year-old child, and many others remember soldiers who died in the 1857 Uprising. Most graves mention the names and the regiments of the soldiers. Mass graves of British soldiers far from home are marked with a poignant "In Memoriam MDCCCLVII. This cross is sacred to the memory of those whose nameless graves lie around."

Where there are graves, there are stories of ghosts, and Lothian cemetery is no different. Anecdotes of wandering spirits are plentiful, but the local favourite is the headless soldier. Jilted by an Indian woman, a British soldier who shot himself at Delhi Gate has reportedly been seen walking all the way from Daryaganj right into the Lothian Cemetery where he is buried. People swear that they have heard him call out his lover's name. True or not, just the sense of his presence hanging in the air is enough to give you the chills.

Address Netaji Subhash Marg, Priyadarshini Colony, Kashmere Gate | **Getting there** Kashmere Gate Metro Station (Red/Yellow Line) | **Hours** Daily, sunrise to sunset | **Tip** Go see the gray granite pillar, the Telegraph Memorial (near Kashmere Gate, British Magazine structure) set up in honour of the workers of the telegraph office, who were able to send the last message out to Ambala Cantonment warning them of the mutiny in Delhi and Meerut. This was why the British were able to quell the Uprising.

64 Madras Coffee House

A vintage hangout for the city's intellectuals

This eatery, situated opposite the Regal Building, across Gate 7 of the Rajiv Chowk Metro station, is never going to win a beauty contest. From its delicately etched silver door to its antique interior, which hasn't changed since 1935, it is definitely a contender for the personality award, however. The old-world charm (which its owners seem adamant on preserving) is unmatchable. It is even more alluring in the context of many heritage establishments shutting down in the colonial Connaught Place market.

The founder of Madras Coffee House, Hem Chand Jain had moved to Delhi from Punjab and opened Shanghai, a Chinese restaurant and bar. Those were the days of the Raj, when jazz clubs were all the rage at Connaught Place. A live band played at Shanghai while British officers danced the night away with their dates. Independence brought with it a time when, like the rest of the country, *Dilliwallahs* too started reclaiming their space. Shanghai's new avatar, Repro Milk Bar, was exclusively vegetarian and didn't serve alcohol. In 1958, when tastes changed and South Indian food became a trend, the restaurant was reborn yet again as Madras Coffee House.

Perhaps it was the freshly brewed filter coffee that lured politicians like Nehru and Indira Gandhi; authors like Khushwant Singh, who read quietly at the table near the counter; and many a famous journalist to this laid-back eatery. A flower-bedecked shrine housing a black idol of Ganesha greets patrons at the door, and plastic flowers, a remnant of the 1970s, still grace the wooden tables. The menu is limited, simple, and authentic. It's a place that does not make an attempt to be liked. And therein lies its charm. Here, couples who want to linger, cash-strapped students, office workers, travellers in search of history, and old-timers with nostalgia-tinged memories bond over *sambhar* (South Indian lentil soup) and coffee.

Address P 5 / 90, Outer Circle, Connaught Place, Tel +91 11 23363074 | **Getting there** Rajiv Chowk Metro Station (Blue / Yellow Line) | **Hours** Daily 11am – 10pm | **Tip** The more popular and expensive Saravana Bhavan, a chain restaurant with satellites in New York and London, serves up South Indian fare.

65___Mandi House & Jor Bagh Metro Stations

Public art on the go

Having changed the landscape of the city, the Delhi Metro is now busy infusing art into the bleak, daily commute. In 2015, the Mandi House and Jor Bagh Metro Stations began donning the garb of art galleries. Through "The Habitat Initiative: Art In Public Spaces," a collaborative effort between India Habitat Centre and the Delhi Metro Rail Corporation (DMRC), the organisation has taken on the task of brightening up gray Metro corridors.

Public art installations are in a nascent stage across India. And though Delhi is the country's art capital, there is a new consciousness about bringing art to the people. It is moving past the formality of national galleries, intimidating contemporary spaces, and hotel exhibits that remain accessible only to an elite few. These efforts, which began with the statues outside RBI (see p. 178) and the more recently installed steel pods at the AIIMS flyover, are finally showing results. The Delhi Metro's art displays are yet another step in the right direction.

The light boxes at both Metro stations are the first phase of community art installations on the mass transit system. When the inaugural display – a series of 20 hand-painted photographs called "The Long Exposure at Udaipur, 1857–1957" – went up at the Jor Bagh Metro Station, harried commuters slowed down a little to take in the images.

It was a similar scene when the Mandi House Metro Station hosted its first exhibit, Tarun Chhabra's dynamic photographs of Basant and Holi festival revelry in Vrindavan. This artistic dialogue at Jor Bagh and Mandi House truly brings art to an audience of commuters. Other metros will soon be joining the ranks of this public art movement. The DMRC announces the schedule of exhibitions every month, creating anticipation for the next show and artist.

Address Jor Bagh Metro Station (Yellow Line), Mandi House Metro Station (Blue/Violet Line), www.delhimetrorail.com | Hours Daily 6am–11pm | Tip India Habitat Centre (Lodhi Road, near Air Force Bal Bharati School, Lodhi Colony, close to Jor Bagh Metro Station) designed by Joseph Stein, is the city's most social space. Its ecological design involves several courtyard spaces, fountains, and beautiful landscaping, which are also parts of the centre's Art in Public Spaces programme.

66 Maulana Azad's Mausoleum

In remembrance of a leader

Muhiyuddin Ahmed Maulana Abul Kalam Azad's (1888–1958) minimalist tomb is in the middle of the Chhata Chowk Bazaar. This freedom fighter and first education minister of India is buried next to the shrine of Hazrat Sarmad Shahid (d. 1661), an Armenian Jew and Sufi poet. Incidentally, Azad had written a beautiful text in 1909 about Shahid.

Habib Rehman, the architect chosen by Nehru to design the tomb, had collaborated with Azad in designing the Lalit Kala Akademi, the Sangeet Natak Akademi, and the Sahitya Akademi. The memorial's modern style is reflective of the India that was being built post Independence. *Drawing from the past but coining a new identity* is the notion reflected upon in Azad's *tafsir* (Qur'anic commentary), which has an entire chapter on *wahdat-i-deen* (unity of religion), written while he was a political prisoner. He would be pleased with the sleek lines of the tomb, which bears a familiar architectural vernacular.

The white marble cross-barrel vault structure starkly contrasts with the red sandstone compound. The mausoleum at the centre echoes the curve of the central arch of the Jama Masjid, which can be seen in the distance. The simple tomb, covered by grass, is deserted and serene. Its peaceful garden looks onto the melee of the street outside, where vendors, rickshaws, and squatters prevail.

Azad's words from his historic address in Ramgarh, in 1940, as the Indian National Congress president, are etched on a black marble plaque: "I am proud of being an Indian. I am part of the invisible unity that is Indian nationality. I am indispensable to this noble edifice and without me this splendid structure of India is incomplete. I am an essential element which has gone to build India. I can never surrender this claim."

Address Meena Bazaar, Chandni Chowk | Getting there Chandni Chowk Metro Station (Yellow Line) | Hours Daily 9am–5pm | Tip The three tall spires on the road near Red Fort mark the Digambar Jain Mandir, also known as Lal Mandir, the oldest Jain temple in Delhi. The impressive carvings, wall paintings, and shrines attract tourists from all over. An avian hospital on the premises treats sick and wounded birds.

67 Metcalfe's Folly
An Englishman's point of view

This stone pavilion perched atop a grassy knoll provides the best view of the huddle of heritage monuments at the Mehrauli Archaeological Park. Dogs roll and children tumble on the turf-covered slope, while old men sit on benches discussing world events and exchanging neighbourhood gossip. It feels quite like the English countryside, and indeed we can attribute this odd structure (and a few others) to the eccentric building patterns of the Englishman Sir Thomas Metcalfe.

Metcalfe's Mehrauli summer house, "Dilkusha," featured several such pavilions. A couple of them are right by the parking lot of the nearby Qutb Minar, one a spiral and the other an odd ziggurat. His pleasure palace was built on Quli Khan's tomb, to which he made several modifications (that have now been reversed). Appointed by the East India Company to deal with the last of the Mughal emperors, Bahadur Shah Zafar, and to oversee civil matters in Delhi, Metcalfe perhaps thought of himself as the next emperor. He even passed off his whimsical additions as a magnanimous gesture towards preserving heritage structures. These structures were also considered a ploy to spy on the Mughal rulers.

Metcalfe's Folly, especially, is an inferior structure. But the view it offers is spectacular – the Qutb Minar looms in the distance; on the horizon you can see Adham Khan's tomb and also the Gurudwara Banda Bahadur. At its feet, the Jamali Kamali tomb and mosque spread out in splendour. Perhaps what Metcalfe lacked in architectural innovation was made up for by commissioning paintings of heritage structures, which are now compiled in *Reminiscences of Imperial Delhi*, or the *Delhi Book*.

Metcalfe's blending of Asian and Occidental architectural styles did not always deliver desired results. But they did bequeath us with this convenient vantage point, and a name that immortalises his eccentric approach.

Address Metcalfe's Folly, Mehrauli Archaeological Park Trail, Christian Colony, Mehrauli | Getting there Qutb Minar Metro Station (Yellow Line) | Hours Daily 7am–5pm | Tip The Jamali Kamali Masjid and tomb, surrounded by a landscaped garden and delicately ornamented coloured tiles, are beautiful structures with a touch of mystery. Jamali was a favoured saint and poet of Emperor Humayun, but the identity of Kamali is lost to history. A romantic theory suggests that he was Jamali's lover.

68_Mirza Ghalib's Haveli
A poet's home

Where there were aesthete emperors, there were legendary court poets. And Delhi is no exception. The Mughals loved their wine, *begums* (Muslim women), and poetry in equal measures. Poetry was, perhaps, accorded more time than even the *begums*. Many celebrated poets have captured the nuances of life under connoisseur emperors in their verses. One such poet is regarded as the most significant contributor in immortalising Urdu poetry; his name is Mirza Ghalib. Centuries later, his lines are worshipped by millions across the country, and flagrantly plagiarised in Bollywood films.

The *haveli* (mansion) where the poet spent his last years, from 1860 to 1869, is a shadow of what it used to be. Ghalib came to live here after the 1857 Uprising, when freedom fighters stormed the capital in protest of the British rule but were beaten back. He wrote some of his most poignant and provocative poetry around this time.

Before the government made some effort in 1997 to create a museum in his memory, this *haveli* had been quartered into small shops selling wood, coal, and building materials. Even if the costumes, hookahs, dinner plates, and *chausar* mat (Indian game) in the musty display cases are all replicas, they serve as the only connection for lovers of Ghalib's fading poetry.

Plaques with Ghalib's *shers* (compositions) in three languages – Urdu, English, and Hindi – pepper the museum. His most poignant couplet, *Hazaaron Khwaishein Aisi ki har khwaish pe dum nikle, Bahut nikle mere armaan, magar phir bhi kam nikle*, translates to: "Thousands of desires, each worth dying for. Many of them I have realized, yet I yearn for more." Reading these makes one wonder about the many nuances lost in translation.

Surely, Asadullah Khan Ghalib would have been amused at the desolate corridors of his *haveli*, for not many visitors come here. And of those who do, very few read or understand Urdu.

Address Gali Qasim Jaan, Ballimaran, Chandni Chowk | **Getting there** Chandni Chowk Metro Station (Yellow Line) | **Hours** Tue–Sun 11am–1.30pm & 2pm–6pm | **Tip** To savour one of Ghalib's favourite foods, step out into the lanes and ask for Ustad Moinuddin kebabs, and be prepared to hear the mixture of spiced meat, zesty lemon, and sweet onion recite poetry on a plate.

69_Mizo Diner

Hip hop and graffiti meet Mizo grub

On the outer edges of Safdarjung, Mizo Diner represents the politically provocative and radical hip-hop movement at the heart of Delhi's thriving alternative scene. A come-as-you-are destination for artists, musicians, and anyone who needs a space to be themselves, this is also the one place where the city's marginalised northeastern population doesn't feel like outsiders, and where they get some finger-licking home-style cooking.

This tiny restaurant can be identified by Kazakh artist Tanai's bold and colourful work on its bare, worn-out concrete steps. The neighbourhood is home to young students and professionals from the seven northeastern states, and the diner has become an after-hours soapbox to discuss geopolitical agendas and cultural identity conundrums. The teal-blue walls of the restaurant serve as a canvas for the owner, David Lalrammawia, aka "Zine," who is also a graffiti and hip-hop artist. The bold stencil graffiti by Bond, the Navi-esque purple woman painted by Artez, and SAMSAM's distinctive figures double as homing beacons for B-Boyers, artists, and musicians.

With its bamboo-clad décor reminiscent of traditional homes in Mizoram, this is the only place where you can sample authentic Mizo fare. The kitchen dishes out unusual delicacies, like *sanpiau* (a congee with crisp fried toppings), and bitter gourd stuffed with shrimp paste; and a few tame dishes, like buffalo steak, grilled chicken, and even a vegetarian *thali* (platter). But the main attraction on the menu is pork – in all its variations – fatty, smoked, fried, stewed, and fermented, all of which go down very well with the strains of hip-hop and Mizo music, and the odd art exhibition, documentary screening, or live music performance thrown in. Naturally, from hipsters and hip-hoppers to street artists and technology nerds, all find this slice of not-so-Delhi exotica quite palatable.

Address 85, Chaudhary Hukum Chand Marg, Humayunpur, Safdarjung Enclave, Tel +91 84475 84361 | Getting there Green Park Metro Station (Yellow Line) | Hours Tue–Sun 11am–11pm | Tip Walk over to the Deer Park near the diner and discover historical tombs from the Mughal era while walking off a few calories from your exotic meal.

70 Museum of Everyday Art
Celebrating the ordinary

Nestled in the steel-and-glass jungle of Gurgaon, the rustic yet contemporary Sanskriti Art Foundation is slightly at odds with its surroundings. This conservatory of crafts so intrinsic to Indian culture is spread over an idyllic five-acre campus in a quiet lane lined by farmhouses. An old banyan tree, planted by Indian classical singing maestro Kumar Gandharva some 25 years ago, plays *darban* (doorman) to the art and cultural complex founded in 1984 by Dr. O.P. Jain.

Over the past few decades, the foundation has evolved into a thriving repository of traditional Indian art forms. However, the star attraction here is the odd and delightful Museum of Everyday Art.

Besides this, it also houses two other museums – the Museum of Indian Textiles and the Museum of Indian Terracotta. The lush campus, once on arid land, also plays home to artists from across India and abroad through an artists' residency program, with eight studios on the premises.

The treasure trove of curiosities and everyday items is just a reminder of the humble origins of art before it went on to become a hallowed field. Inside the museum, the walls are lined with display cases filled with painstakingly chronicled and grouped copper, leather, silver, and wooden household utility objects.

Here, in the golden glow of tungsten filament bulbs, even a spoon or a spice box that would otherwise go completely unnoticed looks like a hallowed object. There's a wonderful collection of metal *paan* boxes and betel-nut crackers, *pujaghars* (altars), uniquely designed coconut graters, pens, and inkwells. These utilitarian artefacts are arranged according to the traditional stages of life as prescribed in Indian scriptures: childhood, academic life, setting up a home, and a spiritual ending (as denoted by items of worship). It's a unique repository that certainly elevates the ordinary to extraordinary.

Address Sanskriti Kendra/Sanskriti Museums, Anandagram, Mehrauli-Gurgaon Road, www.sanskritifoundation.org, info@sanskritifoundation.org, Tel +91 11 26963226 | Getting there Arjangarh Metro Station (Yellow Line) | Hours Tue–Sun 10am–5pm, closed on all public holidays | Tip Check with the Sanskriti office for information about exhibits of resident artists' work, and workshops and lectures on eclectic activities like indigo dyeing, pottery, and metal enameling.

71 Nai Ka Maqbara
The mystery of the barber's tomb

Standing in the shadow of the grand Humayun's Tomb, the Nai ka Maqbara, or Barber's Tomb, is an often overlooked monument. A mere five-minute walk from Humayun's Tomb, this equally impressive grave baffles historians. Buried in the only other structure in the *charbagh* (surrounding garden) of Humayun's Tomb, the remains here must have been those of a very important person; yet no one seems to know why.

What were the events that led an emperor to have his royal barber interred so close by? Who is in the second tomb buried with the barber? Is she his wife? The questions echo in the silence of the far end of the complex where the tomb is situated, close to the tracks of the Nizamuddin Railway Station. The massive platform on which the mausoleum stands is now a playground for scampering squirrels and cooing pigeons, safe in the knowledge that they will not be disturbed. Inside, the two cenotaphs, one for a man and the other for a woman, offer little indication of the identities of those buried. They are both marked with inscriptions from the Quran, and one is marked with the number 999, the *Hijri* year (the year-numbering system used in the Islamic calendar). That would mean that the barber might have been Emperor Akbar's trusted assistant, as the year would be 1590–91, when Akbar was emperor.

In the dark chamber with only the latticed sunlight falling around the grave, one wonders whether the term *nai* (barber) should be taken so literally. Perhaps the tomb was already there, long before the grand tombs came up around it. Was the person who wielded a blade to the emperor's throat so powerful to deserve such an impressive burial site? The grandeur of the double-domed structure and blue-tiled *chattris* (cupolas) only adds to the historical conjecture. Some mysteries may never be solved – or the answers may just be hidden in ancient tomes, waiting to be discovered.

Address Mathura Road, Humayun Tomb Complex | Getting there JLN Metro Station (Violet Line), Pragati Maidan (Blue Line) | Hours Daily, sunrise to sunset | Tip The Neela Gumbad, outside the complex, is the tomb of a slave, built by the poet and nobleman Rahim-i-Rahim.

72_ National Zoological Park

A lone ancient milestone

The Delhi Zoo is one of the country's finest zoological experiences showcasing the continent's flora and fauna. There is also another interesting but deceptively nondescript attraction within its boundaries. Close to the entrance is a Mughal monument that most don't give a second look. The 30-foot-high Kos Minar is a huge conical pillar that stands on a patch of grass cordoned off by a circular gate that always has visitors milling about and perching on it for a better photograph.

The early-17th-century *minar* (tower), one of the many built by Akbar's son Jehangir, is among the few remaining mile markers that were placed every 3 kilometres on major Mughal routes. Made of rubble, masonry, and mortar, and covered with limestone, the medieval *minars* were introduced by Afghan ruler Sher Shah Suri in the 14th century. Later, Akbar, Jehangir, and Shahjahan adopted them to mark approximately 3,000 kilometres of Mughal highways. Some of these even had paintings and inscriptions, but most were just functional and basic in design. Of the few that have survived the ravages of time, three continue to stand in Delhi. The connection between *minars*, *serais* (travellers' inns), and stepwells is recently becoming more evident through restoration efforts.

The milestones provided an efficient communication and espionage system on the dusty routes of the northern plains. It is estimated that 1,000 *minars* marked the miles on the Grand Trunk Road or *Shah Rah-e-Azam* (Great Road), a great continental highway linking the plains of Bengal with Punjab and the North-West Frontier, along which today's modern highways were built. It is easy to imagine the relief a messenger must have felt at the sight of a fresh horse and rider waiting to take over the relay at such a *minar*.

This solitary *minar* evokes a time when these pillars dotted the highways, marking distances to the next *serai* or *baoli* (stepwell). It paints the landscape of a grand empire that once was.

Address National Zoological Park, Mathura Road, www.nzpnewdelhi.gov.in, nzpzoo-cza@nic.in, Tel +91 11 24359825 | **Getting there** Pragati Maidan Metro Station (Blue Line) | **Hours** Apr 1 – Oct 15, Sat – Thu 9am – 4.30pm; Oct 16 – Mar 31, Sat – Thu 9am – 4pm | **Tip** The Old Fort, which borders the Zoological Park, is on the old Grand Trunk Road. Along every fifth *minar*, a *serai* was built by royals, rich merchants, or philanthropists. One can see the old Azimganj Serai currently being restored, along the border of Sunder Nursery and the Zoo.

73__Nau Ghara

A bejewelled temple and nine havelis

The lanes, or galis, of Old Delhi are tiny microcosms of the city. Resplendent *havelis* (traditional mansions), built around central courtyards, hide behind crumbling exteriors and dusty façades. These are homes to communities that have inhabited the walled city since the mid-16th century.

The nine *havelis* or *havelo* of Nau Ghara (literally, "nine homes") comprise one such narrow lane among the old city's maze of streets. They belong to Jain traders who were invited by the Mughal emperor to do business in the thriving capital city, in recognition of their enterprising spirit. With their traditional *jharokhas* (latticed balconies), impressive wooden doorways, and marble staircases, these structures differ from the other old *havelis* of Shahjahanabad. Finely painted vines and flowers (a Persian influence) decorate the bright blue, pink, and yellow entrances of this perfectly preserved enclave.

The three-story *jauhari mandir* (jeweller's temple), known as Indraprastha Tirth Sumatinath Svetambar Jain Temple, at the end of the lane, is as old as the *havelis*, and offers a glimpse into the rich artistic and cultural legacy of Jain temples. The walls of the upper floors are lined with murals and gold filigree work depicting Mughal court life. The roof of the inner sanctum, housing marble statues of *Tirthankars* (perfect souls), is decorated with paintings coloured in natural dyes and finished with gold leaf. The topmost floor hosts mosaic murals made with glass pieces that showcase the life of Lord Mahavir. Keep an eye out for a large idol of the 23rd *Tirthtankar*, Lord Parasnath, made from a rare black *kasauti* stone (touchstone used by jewellers to test the purity of metal).

The heritage enclave of Nau Ghara is a calm oasis in the surrounding chaos. A perfect escape after a few hours spent amid the frenzy of colours, sounds, and smells that is the old city.

Address Nau Ghara, Kinari Bazaar Road, Chandni Chowk | **Getting there** Chandni Chowk Metro Station (Yellow Line) | **Hours** Temple: 6am–1pm & 6pm–8pm. *Havelis* are private homes, so entry is at the discretion of the residents. | **Tip** Refuel at the famous Paranthewali Gali nearby, offering fried flatbread stuffed with all kinds of vegetable fillings and served with generous helpings of butter. Be prepared to wait a little, as this place is always crowded.

74__New Delhi Railway Station Flyover

Neon nights in Delhi

For decades, Paharganj and the area around the New Delhi Railway Station have served as a haven for tourists, providing affordable and accessible accommodation to a community of like-minded travellers. Step outside the station and within moments you will find yourself in a huddle of backpackers.

During the day, the neighbourhood is a gritty tangle of unlit signboards caged in iron grills that hang from shabby hotels lining the dusty roads. By night the cityscape changes dramatically. There is a perceptible shift in energy as the signboards of Paharganj flicker to life. Walking through the byzantine alleyways becomes a quasi-Holi (festival) experience as the neon lights bathe you in a new colour every few feet. Anyone who has stayed here can vouch for the mesmerising effect. Colours from their blinking lights seep in through frosted-glass hotel-room windows, creating a surreal setting that has become a fixation of indie filmmakers wanting to depict the urban underbelly.

Curiously, while cities all over the world are seeing the trend of neon signage on a decline, here, even small hole-in-the-wall businesses and inns revel in the loud, look-at-me quality of the medium. Most will try to convince you that they were the first ones to adopt the trend in 2005.

Internationally, neon has become a medium for artists to express themselves and is now being exhibited in museums. This open-air gallery of lights in Delhi, on the other hand, is a flashy and resplendent arcade of pink, yellows, greens, and blues that remains overlooked and underappreciated.

Here in Paharganj, the language of advertising meets the bold fluorescence of neon, and the result is a photographer's playground.

Address New Delhi Railway Station flyover or Paharganj | Getting there New Delhi
Metro Station (Yellow Line) | Hours Daily 7pm–1pm | Tip Not for Posh Spice types,
restaurants in Paharganj were once the only places where Western cuisine was served with
an unapologetically Indian twist. Shim Tur, a Korean restaurant; Sam's Cafe, a backpackers'
hangout; and Club India Cafe, known for its Japanese food, are three places where you can
tuck in.

75_New Gramophone House
Delhi's vinyl institution

On the fringes of a public jazz concert in Nehru Park, hip youngsters swirl around a table stacked with boxes brimming with record albums. Vinyl, a throwback to the past, is the new cool. Though mass production of these "groovy" black discs stopped in 1992, vinyl is making a huge comeback among the younger generation. For those long smitten by the organic texture of a record's sound and the unpredictable skip of the needle, and for teenagers just awakening to the joys of vinyl, New Gramophone House, located in the pulsating Chandni Chowk, is the go-to place.

For the third-generation owner, Anuj Rajpal, the world still spins at 78 rpm, as it did for his grandfather Bhagwan Dass Rajpal, when the store opened here in 1947. Originally, Rajpal Sr. founded the New Gramophone House in Lahore, Pakistan, in 1930. When he moved to Delhi during India's Partition, he brought his business along with him. Keeping with the times, the New Gramophone House now also has an online shop.

Only the *shaukeen* (connoisseur) finds his way here. A walk up the stairs past a toyshop, garment store, and shoe store is rewarded with the sight of apothecary cabinets brimming with records in all musical genres and languages. From the densely stacked shelves, the attendants can fish 7-inch, 10-inch, or 12-inch records of artists as diverse as Elvis Presley, Begum Akhtar, Mehdi Hassan, Miles Davis, and Kishore Kumar. The upper shelves strain under the weight of antique hand-cranked gramophones, electric turntables, and assorted electronic parts and hardware. The online store caters to patrons around the world in search of an elusive record.

As the newfound obsession for all things retro fuels the demand for an analogue audio experience, naturally the vinyl soundtrack of the popular Hindi movie *Rockstar* takes pride of place among the vintage classics.

Address Shop No. 9, opposite Moti Cinema, Main Road, Chandni Chowk Road, www.ngh.co.in | Getting there Chandni Chowk Metro Station (Yellow Line) | Hours Mon–Sat 10am–9pm | Tip Next to the stairs of the Jama Masjid, the famed Meena Bazaar comes to life in the evening. It's a psychedelic shopping experience with all things glitzy. But if you are still in the mood for music, check out Shop 256, Shah Music Centre.

76__Nigambodh Ghat
The river that once flowed clear

There is no better place to experience the ebb and flow of the river Yamuna than the Nigambodh Ghat, near Ring Road in Delhi. At Jagatpura in North Delhi, fishermen launch their rowboats and buffaloes amble into the water to cool themselves. It's a much gentler river, far from the city's pollution and urban chaos. But at Nigambodh, the ripples of history still pulsate through the waters.

Nigambodh, meaning "realisation of knowledge," comes from the belief that when Lord Brahma regained his lost memory, the Vedas were revealed to him. The Prachin Nili Chhatri Mandir (Ancient Blue Roof Temple), said to have been built approximately 5,300 years ago by King Bharat, is the centre of that faith. Prince Yudhishtira, the eldest of the Pandavas, was purported to have reconstructed the temple, and a 1,000-year-old *shivling* (a representation of Lord Shiva used for worship in temples) was placed here.

The *Imperial Gazetteer of India* once described the water of the Yamuna as "clear blue." Despite the pollution, the river retains its inherent beauty. Boatmen lounge by the shores until they have to push out their boats. A few men while away their time playing cards. During the migratory season, hundreds of birds circle above the calm waters.

The Nigambodh Gate, one of 14 built in Delhi by Emperor Shahjahan, is now just a sandstone skeleton. One of Delhi's oldest cremation ghats, this place used to be constantly alight with funeral pyres until an electric crematorium was built to take on a share of the burden.

The *basti* (settlement) by the river reveres the water, and the city offers *pujas* (prayers). It's not the prettiest river, but the Yamuna imparts a sense of why Delhi grew upon its banks. As Delhi-based author Khushwant Singh wrote, "When life gets too much for you, all you need to do is to spend an hour at Nigambodh Ghat."

Address Near Kashmere Gate, Cremation Ground, Yamuna Bazaar | **Getting there** Kashmere Gate Metro Station (Red/Yellow Line) | **Tip** The Kashmere Gate is one of the most important gates in Delhi. During the Mughal era, the emperor and his entourage used the gate for journeys to Kashmir. It is battle-scarred from the 1857 Uprising, and fortifications were added to it under the British rule.

77—Northern Railways Headquarters

The home of a white Mughal

Just behind St. James Church in the Kashmere Gate area, a large dome of a palatial house dominates the view. In 1803, this was the home of William Fraser, a Scotsman and British East India Company employee who became the Deputy Resident of Delhi in 1823.

Fraser represented the rare breed of British officers who immersed themselves in Indian culture. William Dalrymple's book *City of Djinns* describes Fraser's life in great detail. Fraser read and wrote Persian, had Indian friends, and adopted local clothing and customs. His flamboyant lifestyle included an Indian mistress, evenings with *nautch* girls, flowing liquor, and innumerable hunting expeditions. His life's end was equally intriguing. He was killed in 1835 by an assassin hired by the disgruntled Nawab of Ferozpur, Shamsuddin.

Today, this grand remnant of the Raj is the headquarters of the Chief Administrative Officer (CAO) of Construction for Northern Railways, another British legacy. The dome, though added much later, contributes to its unique architectural appeal. However, the most interesting part of the building – the *tykhanas* (cellars) – is far from prying eyes, as prior permission is required to visit the interior. These ancient *tykhanas* predate Fraser's house, which is built on the former site of Ali Mardan's palace, a senior general and *omrah* (high-ranking courtier) in Shah Jahan's court. Fraser used these underground spaces as cooling rooms in the hot summers.

After sustaining significant damage during the First War of Independence, the house was restored and later received a Heritage Building Award in 1997. If granted permission to tour the property, you will see the octagonal turrets where sentries once stood guard, a portico, and a long driveway. Here, Fraser must have raised many a glass to good times, with the silent Yamuna River as witness.

Address Behind St. James Church, Lothian Road, Kashmere Gate | **Getting there**
Kashmere Gate Metro Station (Red/Yellow Line) | **Hours** Viewable only from outside the
gates | **Tip** St. James Church, commissioned by Colonel James Skinner in 1836, is one of
the oldest churches in Delhi. The crème-coloured structure with its huge dome topped by a
copper ball and cross also houses many tombs of famous British officers, including that of
William Fraser.

78 Old Famous Jalebi Wala
Will the real jalebi please stand up?

Right at the junction of Dariba Kalan, in Chandni Chowk, is Delhi's oldest and most famous *jalebi wallah*. People have been lining up here since 1884, when founder Nemchand Jain put up two oil vats and started piping batter into them. And they just keep coming back for more.

The *jalebis* are made in small batches, and everyone waits until a fresh batch is ready. Among those customers waiting are two distinct categories – the mob and the queue. The crowd surrounding the stand is usually the beneficiary of the current batch. The rest fall in line, waiting for the next round. This is not a process that can be rushed. To those who are patient comes the reward – in the form of piping hot, crunchy *jalebis*. A drizzle of thick *rabri* (sweetened condensed milk) is optional but highly recommended. Most aficionados believe that a heart attack at the Old Famous would be a grand way to go.

Conversation picks up only after the *jalebis* have been polished off. If anyone snaps out of the reverie, it's only because they need to get their wits together to hustle for another serving.

So what's the big deal about this particular deep-fried treat? Unlike the regular tiny *jalebis* that are made from refined flour, the hand-sized *jalebis* at Old Famous are made from lentil flour. The sugar used is a special variety called *khand* (a pure form of sugar), and it is dunked in pure *desi ghee* (clarified butter). The owner is expressionless, efficient, and has the attitude of a French restaurateur who serves just one dish. He is knowledgeable about the *jalebi*, explaining that the *imarti* (a similar fried confection) is Indian, while the *jalebi* was created right here on the streets of Chandni Chowk. However interesting the dish's history may be, the small crush of people outside the shop is only half listening, the looks on their faces akin to that of an addict seeking his next fix.

Address Dariba Kalan, Chandni Chowk | **Getting there** Chandni Chowk Metro Station (Yellow Line) | **Hours** Mon–Sat 10am–8pm | **Tip** To lighten your palate, walk over to Natraj Dahi Balle Wala (1396, Main Road Near Central Bank, opposite Paranthe Wali Gali, Chandni Chowk) and order a plate of spicy *aloo tikki chaat*.

79_Parikrama

Delhi's only revolving restaurant

Typically, reserving a table is not part of the dining-out routine in India. However, at Parikrama, Delhi's only revolving restaurant, you stand to benefit by calling ahead. Otherwise, the waiting time, especially on Sundays, can seriously test your patience. A tip for diners at Parikrama: chew very slowly. It takes an hour and a half for one revolution.

In the city centre, where high-rises are few and far between, a 240-foot-tall structure is, in itself, a reason for celebration. On the 24th floor, the elevator opens into what can only be described as a very classic 1970s decor. As the dining room spins, a slow-motion panorama of Delhi plays out. Signboards in the restaurant point out major landmarks below, like the Jawaharlal Nehru Stadium and the Jama Masjid. At night, the beautifully lit Rashtrapati Bhavan and Sansad Bhavan dominate the skyline. During the day, the meandering Yamuna, awe-inspiring Jama Masjid, peaceful Birla Mandir, and majestic Red Fort draw your attention. Try to spot the Delhi Gate and the revered Gurudwara Bangla Sahib, along with the cluster of neighbouring structures.

Choose from Mughlai, Indian, Indo-Chinese, Thai, and limited Mediterranean fare. It would be wise not to select a fussy dish that is complicated to eat, as this is one place where you would rather focus on the view than the food.

Photography is a major activity of diners, and selfies are the order of the day. The clientele is a mix of families, office colleagues, and couples on a weekly night out. Far above the traffic din, the combination of the dramatic views, the low music, and the quiet murmur of the restaurant (or perhaps the very expensive wine) will leave you giddy – not to mention a few rupees lighter and a few pounds heavier. Eating with your head (and body) in the clouds is a recipe for a happy evening in the heart of Delhi.

Address Antriksh Bhavan, 22, KG Marg, Connaught Place, www.parikramarestaurant.com, Tel +91 11 33106049 | **Getting there** Rajiv Chowk Metro Station (Blue/Yellow Line) | **Hours** Daily 12.30pm–11.30pm | **Tip** The more contemporary Sky Bar & Lounge on the 25th floor hosts a party crowd and has three sections: an open restaurant, a lounge area, and a bar.

80 Parthasarathy Rocks at JNU

Delhi's highest natural point

For those who have read *Jonathan Livingston Seagull* by Richard Bach, watching birds fly around Parthasarathy Rocks will make perfect sense. Within the Jawaharlal Nehru University (JNU) campus, this is a students' haunt (the "cool kids" call it PSR) with geographical significance. JNU is hardly a place where students fall short of open spaces to hang out. Still, the PSR is a favourite spot, especially for the spectacular vista it offers.

The rocks are beneath the flight path of birds as well as airplanes; which is why you will see both avian and aviation enthusiasts with binoculars at all hours. It was named after the first vice chancellor of JNU, G. Parthasarathi. Part of the Aravalli ranges, the trail to the boulder-strewn landscape leads through a wooded area. Older than any man-made structure in Delhi, the Precambrian-era rocks here have been untouched perhaps since the dawn of time. This rocky terrain, it is speculated, has also been a trade route, explaining the ruins in neighbouring locales with names ending in the word *serai* (travellers' inns).

Sunsets and sunrises on the hill are spectacular with the Qutb Minar in plain sight. Amid the drama of nature, an open-air amphitheatre near the rocks often hosts political and arts-related speakers. During the late afternoon, peacocks punctuate the heavy air with piercing cries. *Nilgai* and even porcupines and civets are commonly seen ambling about in the forest. The surrounding grasslands are a safe haven for crested larks, yellow-wattled lapwings, and gray francolins. Towards late evening, groups of students gather to get some fresh air, sneak in a few beers, or just lie under the stars in the foggy city.

There is no better spot to ruminate on life and to watch a Jonathan Livingston Seagull practice his flight.

Address Jawaharlal Nehru University, New Mehrauli Road, Near Munirka | Getting there Hauz Khas Metro Station (Yellow Line) | Hours Sunrise and sunset are recommended times. Birding groups often visit the rocks on Sundays. If visiting alone, it is advisable to be accompanied by a student. | Tip The JNU canteens and *dhabas* (small eateries) have some of the best food in Delhi, at very student-friendly rates.

81 — Qutbuddin Bakhtiyar Kaki's Dargah

The last Mughal emperor's unfulfilled wish

Several paths lead to this oldest *dargah* (shrine) in Delhi, and the most trodden is the road leading down from Gandhak ki Baoli, a stepwell built by Sultan Iltutmish for Hazrat Qutbuddin Bakhtiyar Kaki (1173–1235). The Sufi saint was the successor of Moinuddin Chisti, and the teacher of Fariduddin Ganj-e-Shakar, who, in turn, was the mentor of the Sufi saint Nizamuddin Auliya.

Before Qutb Sahib (a name by which Hazrat Kaki is known) came to Delhi, the Sufi tradition was restricted to Ajmer and Naguar. His *dargah* has seen many additions since it was built, mostly by individuals seeking blessings from the saint. Aurangzeb's floral tiles decorate a wall in the *dargah*. Shaikh Khalil, a descendant of Qutb Sahib's successor, built the northern gate, and Aurangzeb's son Bahadur Shah I erected the stately Moti Masjid nearby.

The gentle breeze and the rustle of trees within the *dargah* calm even the noisiest of followers. The pious kneel in supplication and the needy tie threads to the marble screen, asking for wishes to be fulfilled. Consider it a divine grace shining down upon you if you chance upon a lone *qawwal* (singer) offering his song at the shrine.

It is believed that those buried alongside the grave of a Sufi saint will be allowed to cross into the gates of paradise on judgement day. Commoners and kings, *fakirs* and noblemen, all hold this to be true and have their graves next to Hazrat Kaki's. In a compound accessible through the Ajmeri Gate are the graves of emperors Bahadur Shah I, Shah Alam II, and Akbar II. The last Mughal emperor, Bahadur Shah Zafaralso, also had hoped to be buried here, but was banished for his role in the 1857 Uprising. He remained in exile, in faraway Rangoon, till the end of his days. A vacant plot in the graveyard still awaits his remains.

Address Haveli Ladho Sarai, Mehrauli | Getting there Qutb Minar Metro Station (Yellow Line) | Hours Daily, sunrise to sunset | Tip Zafar Mahal (Gandhi Colony, Mehrauli), the emperor's summer residence, is the last palace built by Mughal rulers. The sandstone structure used to be called Jungli Mahal because of the forest and wilderness that surrounded it back then.

82 Rai Lala Chunnamal's Haveli

The largest haveli in Old Delhi

Looking up from the bustling street market at one of the largest, still lived-in *havelis* (mansions) in Shahjahanabad, you can plainly see the ravages of time. Despite the huge transformer that partially covers the façade, it is hard to miss the grand building with its red-trimmed doors and green shutters. The ground floor that once housed the large kitchens of this three-storey, 128-room house is now a huddle of dilapidated shops. The stairway, with its brass balustrade, leads to a small courtyard on the first floor. Another staircase leads to a terrace, offering excellent views of Katra Neel and Chandni Chowk.

Built in 1848 by textile merchant Rai Lala Chunnamal, the *haveli* was once the centre of political and business activity. At a time when everyone in the country was choosing sides, Chunnamal, an astute businessman, decided to ally with the British. They appointed him the first municipal commissioner of Delhi, conferring upon him the title Rai. His salary of 100,000 rupees made Chunnamal the richest man in the city. He was the first Indian in Delhi to install a telephone and buy a car. He also owned the city's first theatre.

Anil Preshad, a 10th-generation descendent of Chunnamal, still lives in the *haveli* with his family. The Preshads, who are courteous and welcoming, have seen their fair share of visitors, dignitaries, and curious individuals who accidentally stumble upon this building. Actor Kate Winslet is framed for posterity in a photograph in the palatial 50-foot-long drawing room. With its silk-lined ceiling, gilded mouldings, baroque mirrors, Belgian chandeliers, and fireplace mantels displaying both historical photographs and private memorabilia, the hall evokes the feeling that one is intruding upon a family's personal story, but a story that's intertwined with the history of Delhi.

Address Dariba Nukkad, Katra Neel, Chandni Chowk | **Getting there** Chandni Chowk Metro Station (Yellow Line) | **Hours** Depends on the owner | **Tip** Enjoy a *banta* (lemon soda) at Pandit Ved Prasad Lemonwale (Shop No. 5466, near Town Hall, Chandni Chowk), the supposed pioneer of this drink.

83_Rajon ki Baoli

The prettiest and largest stepwell

Among the splendid monuments that dot the archaeological ruins of Mehrauli, the first ancient city of Delhi, is a *baoli* (stepwell) built for masons in the 16th century, during the Lodhi era, by Daulat Khan. The *baoli* doesn't get many visitors, even though the Qutb Minar, which is just around the corner, is one of Delhi's most popular attractions. Locals know it as *sookhi baoli* (dry well), a practical name since this not-so-deep well has long since dried up.

In this parched city, *baolis*, some dating back nearly 700 years, are still used for their primary function: as a source of water. Making provisions for water in the form of these wells was an essential part of the governance strategy for any ruler who wished to succeed in Delhi. While some are decrepit, and others with water unfit for use, these wells offer a glimpse into the life of commoners as opposed to kings.

What Rajon ki Baoli lacks in functionality, it makes up for in aesthetics. It retains architectural elements of the graceful Lodhi style. Along the perimeters of the three steps are open chambers with perfect trabeated arches, providing shelter to siesta seekers, reminiscent of an era when traders and travellers used *baolis* as resting places. Stairways on both sides lead to a terrace where a mosque and a tomb share space.

Until very recently, *baolis* were a zealously guarded city secret. But the phenomenal success of the Bollywood blockbuster *PK*, in which the protagonist uses one such *baoli* as his shelter, has put *baolis* on the tourist map. Fortunately, the movie was not shot at Rajon ki Baoli – and that is why you can still read a book, take a nap, chat with friends on the broad steps, or just while away the hours sitting in the cool interiors doing nothing.

The nonchalant peacocks in the complex are seldom bothered by the few visitors who find their way here.

Address Mehrauli Archaeological Park, Garhwal Colony, Mehrauli | **Getting there** Qutb Minar Metro Station (Yellow Line) | **Hours** Daily, sunrise to sunset | **Tip** Walking down to the Mehrauli village to the right of the Rajon ki Baoli will bring you to Gandhak ki Baoli, which is still in use. Enjoy the sight of children diving, women washing clothes, and men loitering around this sulphur-infused stepwell.

84__Razia Sultan's Tomb
The shambles of Delhi's first female ruler

Is the real burial site of Razia Sultan, beloved daughter of Sultan Shamsuddin Iltutmish, in Old Delhi? Or is it in Tonk, Rajasthan? Or in Siwan, Haryana? Fiercely disputed by historians, the "official" tomb is recognised to be in Pahari Bhojla in Old Delhi, accessed through lanes lined by convenience stores, butcher shops, sleeping goats, *chaiwallahs*, and biryani joints.

A spartan mosque flanks the open-air grave. Devout men offer *namaz* (prayers) beside the tomb of a woman who loved, ruled, and fought with passion. The neighbouring tomb is said to be of Razia's little-known sister, Shazia. This simple grave made of rubble masonry, and set in the midst of everyday life, is an anti-climax for Delhi's only female ruler, who refused to be called *Sultana* because it implied being the "wife of a Sultan," whereas she was an empress in her own right.

Artists have distilled historic notes and documents into vignettes of her extraordinary yet tragic life, presented in television shows, plays, and books. She took an interest in the affairs of state early on, dressed like a man, and didn't cover her face, which her non-Muslim subjects found endearing, but which alienated her from Muslims. Razia irked noblemen with radical views about abolishing taxes on non-Muslims. She ruled Delhi from 1236 to 1240, until her brothers and court nobles thwarted her reign and ultimately vanquished her.

As a 13th-century Persian historian states, "Sultan Raziya was a great monarch. She was wise, just, and generous, a benefactor to her kingdom, a dispenser of justice, the protector of her subjects, and the leader of her armies. She was endowed with all the qualities befitting a king, but she was not born a man, and for that reason, in the estimation of men, all these virtues were worthless." There is no classical beauty to the Sultan's tomb, yet its austerity seems just right.

Address Shahi Masjid, Bulbuli Khana, Pahari Bhojla | Getting there Chandni Chowk Metro Station (Yellow Line) | Hours Daily, sunrise to sunset | Tip Turkman Gate is one of the 14 gates of Shahjahanabad. It is named after a 13th-century Sufi known as Shams-ul-Arifeen Shah Turkman Byabani, who died in 1240, the same year as Razia Sultan.

85__ Reserve Bank of India
Delhi's first public art installation

The high-security building of the Reserve Bank of India, the central banking institution of the country, on Sansad Marg, would not seem the likeliest place to find works of art on public display. Yet the two towering sentinels that flank the entrance of this financial establishment are quite fitting: they are the mythical attendants of Kuber, the god of wealth.

When Prime Minister Jawaharlal Nehru proposed that art flourish alongside public buildings of independent India, the bank set up a committee to select work befitting its stature. The committee came up with the idea of two sculptures to represent prosperity through industry and agriculture. J R D Tata, who was a director on the central board, advised the committee to seek the counsel of art critic Carl Khandalawalla, who in turn recommended figures of a Yaksha and a Yakshini, as they appealed on mythological, modern, and artistic levels.

Nine artists were solicited to submit proposals, and it was noted sculptor Ram Kinkar Baij whose idea was selected. Baij drew from the derivative form of Parkham Yaksha in the museum of Mathura and Bisnagar Yakshini in the Kolkata museum. He took his time to select the perfect material and transport it. In the process, he missed many deadlines, and effectively held the bank hostage to his extremely creative whims.

Once finished, the sculptures created ripples not only in the art world, but also in political circles. The Rajya Sabha (upper house of the Indian Parliament) has a record of one member, Professor Satyavrata Siddhantalankar, questioning the objective behind erecting the statue of a naked woman in front of the grand Reserve Bank of India.

If you choose to look beyond the disconcertingly perfect bosom of the Yakshini, it's clear that Baij's talent is as immense as his sculptures, which remain among the very few public installations in the city.

Address 6, Sansad Marg, Sansad Marg Road Area | **Getting there** Patel Chowk Metro Station (Yellow Line) | **Hours** The view from the road is available at all times. Entry is restricted. | **Tip** Check out some rare stamp collections, including the first Indian postage stamps released in 1854, at the National Philatelic Museum (Dak Bhavan, Sardar Patel Chowk, Sansad Marg, Mon–Fri 10am–5pm). You can even get your photograph converted into your own personal stamp.

86__Rikhi Ram Musical Instruments

Sitar maker to the Beatles

During the pre-Partition era, Rikhi Ram, a young music enthusiast from Lahore, ran a music shop in the city's Anarkali Bazaar and moonlighted at a museum, where he looked after the upkeep of the musical instruments. His passion prompted accomplished musicians like Abdul Harim Poonchwale and Ramzan Khan to teach him the art of making instruments.

When Rikhi Ram came to Delhi in the 1920s, he opened a music store in the city's oldest market, the Gole Market. Three generations later, this shop continues to be the soul of the local music community. Glass cabinets lining the front half of the store showcase a variety of instruments, each one bearing the unmistakable stamp of craftsmanship: the sheen on a *sitar*, the heft of a *sarod*, the curves of a guitar. The smoothly aged benches in the cove invite you to take in the museum-like ambience. On the wood-panelled walls, images of legends from classical Indian music rub shoulders with rock royalty – united in their patronage of Rikhi Ram's. A customer banters with the shop assistant, while Ajay (one of Rikhi Ram's sons) strings a newly-made sitar.

There's a sense that anything could happen at Rikhi Ram's. Like when the Beatles strolled into the store in 1966 and picked up a few instruments. They were here on recommendation from Peter Sellers, the legendary Hollywood actor. Rikhi Ram's had come to Sellers' rescue when he needed a sitar for a film. The fuss being made by the crowd that followed the Beatles must have been amusing to the man who was used to catering to the musical greats of the country. When maestros Ustad Fayyaz Khan Saheb, Ustad Bade Ghulam Ali Khan Saheb, and Pt. Omkarnath Thakur visited, the sound of them tuning their instruments would have floated out to the street. And you never know when Herbie Hancock – or Bill Gates – might visit again.

Address G-8, Marina Arcade, Connaught Place, www.rikhiram.in, info@rikhiram.com, Tel +91 11 23340496 | Getting there Rajiv Chowk Metro Station (Blue / Yellow Line) | Hours Daily 9am – 9pm | Tip Wenger's (A 16, Connaught Place) is one of Delhi's oldest bakeries. Everyone has at one time bought a birthday cake from this local institution. The seasonal fresh fruit pastry is their biggest draw.

87__Roshanara Bagh
The pleasure garden of a banished princess

Once upon a time, there lived a princess who found herself in the eye of a political storm within her family. She sided with her favourite brother, Mohyuddin Muhammed Aurangzeb, in the fight. What happened next, as they say, is history. This is the story of Roshanara, the daughter of Mumtaz Mahal and Shah Jahan, emperor of India from 1628 to 1658 and the builder of the Taj Mahal.

Though history has a biased telling, it is fair to say that Roshanara lived in a time where royal families were always torn into factions, shredded by hatred, and blinded by power. With shrewd foresight and evil machinations, Roshanara made sure that her brother Dara Shikoh – the emperor's first choice for the heir apparent – was executed, the emperor was imprisoned, and her chosen brother, Aurangzeb, secured the throne.

Perhaps history would have judged Roshanara differently for her ambition, intelligence, vanity, and greed, if she were a man. She ruled Aurangzeb's kingdom and his harem, had multiple lovers, and worked administrative affairs to her gain, until complaints about her provocative lifestyle started tumbling in.

As a staunch Muslim, Aurangzeb disagreed with her libertine ways and banished her to Roshanara Bagh. Amid this palace's garden, which resembled paradise, Roshanara the poet continued her bohemian existence. Her untimely end, and her lover's, was caused by poison. Following her death, she was interred here. Whispers in the garden still hide the secret of who murdered Roshanara.

Today, Roshanara Bagh is the only tangible memory of the princess. The palace, with its shallow moat, dry fountains, and half-kempt gardens hosts family picnics, kids' cricket games, and lazing loiterers. A marble screen in the centre of the open *baradari* (pavilion) shields the tomb from the harsh judgement that the princess's life might elicit from visitors.

Address Roshanara Bagh, Roshanara Road, near Kamla Nagar Clock Tower and Old Sabzi Mandi | Getting there Pulbangash Metro Station (Red Line) | Hours Daily, sunrise to sunset | Tip On the northern ridge stands the Mutiny Memorial (Rani Jhansi Marg, Civil Lines), a neo-Gothic tower built in honour of the soldiers of the Delhi Field Force who fought the 1857 Uprising.

88__The Sari School

The fall, drape, and pleat of an ancient garment

Though the sari is ubiquitous in India, most young urban women don't wear them; many don't even know how to drape the nine yards of fabric. Over the years, this unstitched garment has become relegated to special-occasion wear, to be worn only at weddings and traditional events. Enter the Sari School, a unique institution started in 2009 by sari historian and expert Rta Kapur Chisti, a dedicated advocate of handlooms in India. At the heart of the school is the desire to inform individuals about the rich diversity of textiles, patterns, and spinning and weaving techniques in the hopes of reviving appreciation for the art and tradition of the sari.

On most Saturday afternoons, the basement studio space of Chisti's Taanbaan design label in the up-and-coming neighbourhood of Jangpura transforms into a sari workshop, where groups of women spend three hours grappling with fussy folds and mastering new methods. Some of them have never worn a sari, while others hope to experiment with modern styles of draping, a trend that Chisti feels will be the way forward if the sari is to survive.

Knowing the origins of a sari are essential to understanding the garment and its evolution. Visual aids weave a story of culture and tradition, introducing participants to the different incarnations of saris in India's states. Chisti peppers the class with delightful nuggets of information, like the fact that the practice of wearing petticoats and blouses underneath saris was introduced towards the beginning of the 19th century in response to western notions of etiquette and decorum.

In one corner, a young woman almost gives up, defeated by the pleats; in another, a few foreign visitors practice winding themselves up in bundles of cloth. In contrast, the style divas of the group quickly learn to confidently convert the sari into pants, gowns, and even shorts. All participants practice at least four draping styles.

Address K-42, Jangpura Extension, www.anandakhadi.com/sari_school.html,
Tel +91 11 41823927 (10am−6pm) | Getting there Jangpura Metro Station (Violet Line) |
Hours Sat 2.30pm−5.30pm | Tip Kabul (Shop No. 4/8, near Kashmiri Park, opposite
Modi Pastry, Bhogal, Central Rd, Jangpura Extension) is a one-stop destination for
authentic Afghani food.

89__Satpula

A bridge across history

Is it a bridge, a dam, or a first line of defence? Well, the Satpula dam, as it is commonly known, is all of this and more. Although it's quite visible from the road, many dismiss the stone ramparts as a wall, but the Satpula, part of the city of Jahapanah, is, in fact, one of the few waterworks commissioned by Muhammad bin Tughlaq, the Turkic Sultan of Delhi (reigned 1325 – 1351). The existence of a massive ancient bridge or dam would seem incongruous on the Press Enclave Road, but then again, this is Delhi, a "city of cities." Water was, and still is, Delhi's Achilles heel; and the provisions made for water have always determined a ruler's success.

This two-storey structure is an impressive testimony to the engineering skills and strategy of a conqueror, and his determination to strengthen and expand his kingdom. The dam was built on a local stream that flowed into the Yamuna, and wooden sluices controlled the stored water, alleviating severe drought conditions in the surrounding farming areas. It is said that traces of this reservoir extend between the edges of Khirkee, Chirag Dilli, and Sheikh Sarai.

The ramparts look down on a flat green patch of land where local boys play cricket. In the evening sun, the masonry takes on a deep red hue and its stones and bricks provide a good scratching post for a pack of dogs, the self-appointed guardians of the dam. On a broad pavilion, a gated madrassa serves as a hangout for children. The small, almost dry pond beyond attracts water buffaloes, birds, butterflies, and even a few horses.

As with all ancient Delhi sights, the folklore of the waters curing all ills exists here too, as the Sufi saint Nasiru'd-Din Mahmud, also known as Chiragh-i-Delhi ("Lamp of Delhi") performed *wuzu* (a cleansing ritual) before *namaz* (prayers) in these waters. The waters dried up long ago, but the area still serves as an interesting detour.

Address Main Press Enclave Road, Saket | Getting there Malviya Nagar Metro Station (Yellow Line) | Hours Mon–Sat 10am–6pm | Tip MGF Metropolitan Mall (A-2, Press Enclave Marg, District Centre, Saket) and Select City Walk (A-3, District Centre, Saket) are perfect for shopaholics looking to indulge in some retail therapy.

90__The Second-Largest Flag in India

Standing tall in the heart of Delhi

Fluttering in the wind, belying its weight of over 35 kilograms, the second-largest Indian flag stands at the centre of the heritage Central Park premises at Connaught Circle. The sight of this glorious national banner is enough to evoke patriotic feelings in even the most cynical of Indians. Flying right in the heart of Luytens' Delhi, it is an unabashed tribute to the sacrifices that freedom fighters made to overthrow more than 100 years of British rule.

Children, particularly, are huge fans of this recent addition to the Connaught Circle urban landscape. Every day, scores of students on school outings scramble through the gates and tumble onto the lawns of Central Park. The faces of these little ones beam with pride as they salute this mammoth emblem of India's identity. Adult tourists are more restrained in their display of nationalistic fervour, alternating between craning their necks to take one more look, pretending to read nuggets of information inscribed on the plaques around the flag, and vying for the best angle to frame the flag in their viewfinders.

Naveen Jindal's Flag Foundation of India installed the flag on March 7, 2014, in collaboration with the New Delhi Municipal Council. Spanning 60 feet in height and 90 feet in length, this is among the largest national flags, and is hoisted on a 207-foot-high mast. The mast even has a small port door, and one wonders if there is a tiny ladder within it that leads to the top. This is one of the few flags in India that is not lowered at sunset, as per the rules of the Flag Code. Special permission allows this monumental flag to continue flying at night on the condition that it is always lit. Eight 2,000-watt lights make it a sight to behold after a tiring evening spent shopping around Connaught Circle.

Address Central Park, Connaught Place | **Getting there** Rajiv Chowk Metro Station (Yellow Line) | **Hours** All day | **Tip** Palika Bazaar, an air-conditioned market, operates in the underground complex below Central Park, offering retail therapy at pocket-friendly prices.

91 Sharma Farms
A farm of antique furniture

The farmhouses on the outskirts of Delhi have always belonged to the elite. The rural getaways of Lucullan chateaus or *haveli*-styled mansions, with Olympic-sized pools, are famous as party havens or second homes. Sharma Farms is an antique furniture emporium hidden away in one such small enclave near Tivoli farms in Chhatarpur. Owner Sharmaji is rumoured to be a collector who opened his doors to the public, and most regulars feel blessed that he did so.

Antiquing enthusiasts come to a massive open warehouse in search of great finds at bargain prices. At the entrance you'll find a 30-foot snake boat, once part of the ancient annual boat-racing tradition known as *Vallam Kali* (literally "boat game") in Kerala; try and walk by it with a straight face. Be prepared to not look impressed by the imposing Buddha statues thrice the height of an average human.

There is an ad hoc categorisation of items and a semblance of aisles. The first warehouse is filled with garish carved silver chairs, marble tabletops with lion paws as feet, and mirrored furniture. Rows of decorative doors, gazebos, pillars, and statues of elephants, lions, Gandhi's three monkeys, and laughing Buddhas are followed by innumerable wardrobes, cabinets, and dressers. It's an endless parade of four-poster beds, bar stools, trunks, wheels, candlesticks, and various bits and bobs. The metal, leather, and stoneware sections are filled with pots, pans, and other interesting items that one might want to possess, but it takes some imagination to find their purpose. If something catches your fancy, a small office at the entrance is there to serve you, but browsers are left to their own devices.

It may take some time, but you're as likely to find objects common to homes in South India as to monasteries in Ladakh. Heritage items from every Indian state are among the trove of treasures sold here.

Address Dera Gaon Road, near Chhatarpur Mandir | Getting there Chhatarpur Metro Station (Yellow Line) | Hours Daily 10am–6pm | Tip Chhatarpur Temple used to be the largest temple complex in Delhi before Akshardham stole its thunder. One of Delhi's most popular temples, Chhatarpur is an awe-inspiring yet bizarre rendition of several architectural styles.

92__Shri Ram Centre for Performing Arts

The brutalist trail

It's an odd building: balanced on two cylindrical barrels is a cube that looks like it might topple over at any moment. Designed by architect Shiv Nath Prasad, Shri Ram Centre for Performing Arts (SRCPA) is one of Delhi's landmark structures. In the middle of the theatre district at Mandi House, it is one of the leading theatre schools. Inside the unique space, actors perform, study, and rehearse plays as complex as the building itself.

After Independence, Delhi became the centre of a fresh vision that was slowly taking shape, and the Indian government commissioned several public buildings. Leaders in design, architecture, engineering, and construction were building a new Delhi, free and proud. Prasad, influenced by the Le Corbusier aesthetic, displayed his architectural prowess in SRCPA's brutalist form. A stark and functional style of architecture that emerged in the 1950s, brutalism is an offshoot of modernism that is defined by its massive geometric forms and use of raw, rugged materials, such as poured concrete.

There is an intense energy about the stage where actors repeat lines until the tone, timbre, and feeling resound within themselves and the theatre. The performance spaces are all mostly in the cylindrical portions, and offer an intimacy between audience and performers. The cubic structures include space for rehearsal, and the boundaries between outside and inside are blurred. A small cafe and a narrow path with a low gate lend a charming counterpoint to this severe building.

Many consider the sculptural style crude, but the Shri Ram Centre for Performing Arts is considered one of the finest examples of brutalist architecture in the world. Theatre buffs can look forward to watching spectacular plays performed by some of the best Hindi actors at the centre.

Address 4, Safdar Hashmi Marg, Mandi House, www.shriramcentre.org, shriramcentre@srcpa.in, Tel +91 11 23714307 | Getting there Mandi House Metro Station (Blue/Violet Line) | Hours Check for play listings | Tip Walk down Barakhamba Road to see some beautiful bungalows reflective of the colonial British style. High-rises seem to be closing in on any available space, making the last civil residences from the Lutyens era an endangered species.

93 Southex Books and Prints

Antique books, maps, prints, and photographs

A quiet residential area in South Extension is home to one of the country's best antiquarian bookstores. Nothing prepares you for the drama of the old colonial decor of Southex Books and Prints. Among the neat rows of prints, parchment, and leather-bound books, only the marble-top counters give away that this is a place of business which attracts passionate bibliophiles from around the world.

It all began in the mid-1980s, when a Parsi doctor from Bombay asked antique dealer G C Jain to purchase his entire book collection along with his antique furniture. While seeking buyers for the books, Jain realised that these were rare finds that had value and a market. Today, as one of the 50 dealers in antiquarian books and art in India, Southex sells to institutions, embassies, auction houses, and private collectors. Its speciality is 18th- and 19th-century works that capture the European zeal for discovering the culture, tradition, and customs of a new land.

Lined with wall-to-wall and floor-to-ceiling wooden shelves, Southex looks like a private den. To be seated in the warm light of the chandeliers, in the strangely familiar vintage armchairs, surrounded by rare books, maps, lithographs, and photographs, is a precious feeling. Aquatints of every known flora and fauna in the Indian subcontinent, meticulously categorised by explorers, are also available.

The rare *Oriental Scenery*, by Thomas and William Daniell, is the most expensive volume in their collection. A mint-condition copy of this book would be priced at one crore rupees (10 million). Other treasures include the first English translation of *The Kama Sutra*, by Vatsyayana, an extremely rare first edition of *Lolita*, by Vladimir Nabokov, and a copy of *The Ascent of Everest*, by John Hunt, signed by all expedition members, including Sir Edmund Hillary.

Address A-40, NDSE, South Extension Part II, www.southexbooksandprints.co.in, southexbooksprints@gmail.com, Tel +91 11 26257095 | **Getting there** AIIMS Metro Station (Yellow Line) | **Hours** Mon–Sat 10.30am–6pm, by appointment preferred | **Tip** A 15th-century mosque called Moth ki Masjid, constructed by Lodhi's prime minister, is near the mostly residential South Extension area.

94__St. John's Church

A Mughal façade, a cross, and a temple spire

Walking along the perfectly trimmed hedges and neat rows of spring blooms, you could mistake the sandstone façade flanked by stone ramparts and adorned with calligraphic etchings for a Mughal monument. Squint a bit and the sight of a squat Christian cross above what looks like a white spire of a Hindu temple throws you off completely. Situated in a narrow blink-and-you-miss-it lane of Christian Colony in Mehrauli, a stone's throw away from Qutb Minar, this amalgam of religious iconography is a unique representation of India's ability to absorb cultures and belief systems.

Any chat with the locals about the church invariably leads to recollections of annual grand processions of the cross that were organised decades ago. The church also used to be a pit stop for the multi-religious *Phool Walon Ki Sair* (procession of flower sellers), an annual festival in Mehrauli.

The design of the church is based on that of St. John's College, Agra. James Collins, author of *Context, Culture and Worship: The Quest for 'Indian-ness,'* shares the story of how a tongawalla, too lazy to take a foreign tourist to Akbar's tomb in Sikandra, instead brought the unsuspecting traveller to St. John's College. One wonders whether Rev. Alfred Coore, the designer of the church, was indeed inspired by Akbar's esoteric Din-i Ilahi religion, which was based on various religions.

Built in 1928, the interiors of this church have been renovated over time. If locked, friendly locals holler for the gardener, who fetches the key from the residents who stay in the church compound. The concrete interior, housed in the original courtyard, is lined with arched chambers in Mughal architectural style. A climb up the stairs through the temple spire – a watchtower of sorts – leads to the terrace with its breathtaking view: the Qutb Minar, seemingly within touching distance.

Address St. John's Church Compound, Christian Colony, Mehrauli | **Getting there** Qutb Minar Metro Station (Yellow Line) | **Hours** Daily, sunrise to sunset | **Tip** Get lost in the maze called Bhul Bhulaiyya that marks the tomb of Adham Khan, which is at the junction of the Mehrauli bus stand as you come out of the lane of St. John's Church.

95___St. Martin's Garrison Church

The soldiers' church

At first glance, the square church, located on Raisina Hill, looks like something made out of Legos. Except this behemoth took three and a half million locally-made red Roman bricks to build. Completed in the 1930s for 17,000 euros, St. Martin's Garrison Church is one of only two buildings designed in India by Arthur Shoosmith, an Anglo-Russian architect who was part of Edward Lutyens' team, which built New Delhi.

In keeping with the minimalist theme of the building, a few bare trees frame the exterior of the church with its square towers. The lack of windows served to keep out the summer heat and also indicates the former military use of the church, which looks more like a stockade or fort.

The huge interior dome, which remains invisible from the outside, is typical of a basilica's structural form, but the resemblance ends there. Shoosmith employed a classical-meets-vernacular yet urban architectural design. This is evident in the use of unadorned bricks, reflecting a European aesthetic.

Within the cool interior of the St. Martin's Garrison Church, the echoes of an Easter service attended by Lord Mountbatten, the last Viceroy of India, and his wife, Lady Edwina, in 1947, the last year of the British Empire in India, still linger. To this day, the church continues a tradition started in 1958 of holding a special service on Remembrance Day. Armed forces personnel attend this service irrespective of religion.

Peaceful as it is, the solemnity of the church speaks to you in its starkness; this is a truly unusual structure among the buildings of the British Empire in India. The only voices filtering through this sacred space are the children gambolling on the playground outside.

Address Church Road, Birjlal Dua Marg, Pratap Chowk, Delhi Cantonment | Getting there Dhaula Kuan Metro Station (Orange Line) | Hours Sunday Service: 8.30am in summer, 9am in winter | Tip The Rashtrapati Bhavan, the official residence of the President of India, requires prior approval for admission, but the areas that are open to the public are a great example of the convergence of several architectural styles.

96_ St. Xavier's School

Previously the Cecil Hotel

Back in 1875, this plantation-style hotel of 100 rooms was said to be exclusively for the whites, where the British gentry got caught up over leisurely lunches and idle gossip. When the Society of Jesus (Jesuits) bought the Cecil Hotel in 1959 for 19 lakh rupees from its American owners, they were given a couple of conditions to ensure the preservation of the hotel's architecture. The Jesuits have honoured their promise. Much of the original hotel, with its Victorian columns, arches, wood floors, planters, and bathroom fittings bearing the "Royal Doulton, Made in England" stamps, still harks back to the old days.

Although the memory of the Cecil might be sepia-tinged, stories of a plush hotel with rambling gardens and lawns, and the best swimming pool in the region, live on. For many first-time visitors to India, after days on a ship, the hotel would have been a refuge from the heat and the dust.

The Cecil was especially popular among visiting foreign press correspondents, who sometimes lived there for months on end. The non-fiction book *Diapers on a Dateline: The Adventures of a United Press Family in India During the 1950s* captures the lives of journalists who made the hotel their home. In *An Indian Summer*, author James Cameron reminisces about his stay at the Cecil in 1946, when his room opened onto a courtyard with a pool in which water lilies grew. He revisited it in the 1970s to find his old room turned into a classroom.

The old graduates of St. Xavier's remember their classrooms having attached baths when it first opened in the 1960s, but the school has added more buildings for academic use since then. The Cecil Hotel was declared a heritage structure in 1997. Although now mostly out of bounds to the students, the original building continues to house the library, heritage hall, and residences for the Jesuit priests.

Address 4, Raj Niwas Marg, www.stxaviersdelhi.com | Getting there Civil Lines Metro Station (Yellow Line) | Hours During school hours (certain areas are off-limits). Prior permission necessary. | Tip Peruse the photographs in the Curzon room at Maidens, the oldest hotel in Delhi (7, Sham Nath Marg, Civil Lines). They are sure to transport you to the days of the Raj.

97__State Bank of India
The erstwhile palace of a nautch girl

The three-storey State Bank of India (SBI) building, with its 70-foot-high Palladian façade, towering colonnades, and arches, stands unassuming yet proud on the main thoroughfare of Chandni Chowk. A signboard outside traces the history of this heritage structure from its beginnings as the palace of one of India's most romanticised female mercenaries to its conversion into the Imperial Bank by the British in 1847, to its present role as a branch of the country's most prolific bank.

Akbar Shah II gifted the palace to the politically influential Begum Samru in 1806. Shaper of many a destiny in the Mughal and British courts, Begum Samru went by several names (Farzana-i-Aziza, Zeb-un-nissa, Begum Joanna Nobilis Sombre). Her transformation from a dancing girl in Old Delhi's Chawri Bazaar into a prominent power broker is a fascinating tale of love and political ambition.

Walter Reinhardt, a German mercenary, became enamoured of Farzana, then a 14-year-old dancer, and married her. As Reinhardt moved from one ruler to another, Farzana helped him make shrewd political decisions. After the death of Reinhardt, Begum Samru became the ruler of the province of Sardana in Meerut, commanding its mercenary army. She left a vast fortune that is disputed to this day by an organisation called Reinhards Erbengemeinschaft, whose members are descendants of the Reinhardt bloodline.

Today, the palace celebrates its banking heritage more than the story of its historic occupant. Amidst a series of photographs tracing the evolution of the palace, there's just one portrait of this petite, feminist dancer-turned-warrior; and it presents her as an 80-year-old matriarch wearing her trademark turban and smoking a hookah. The rest of the museum is dedicated to the history of banking. Historians and novelists, though, continue to be fascinated by the invincible mercenary.

Address 1494–95, S. M. E., Chandni Chowk Road, Tel +91 11 66166010 | Getting there Chandni Chowk Metro Station (Yellow Line) | Hours Mon–Sat 10am–5pm | Tip A few minutes away, the Gurudwara Sis Ganj (near Red Fort, Chandni Chowk Road), the spot where Guru Teg Bahadur (ninth of the ten Gurus of the Sikh religion) was martyred by Emperor Aurangzeb, is an important part of Sikh history.

98__Subz Burj

A 15th-century traffic circle

The Subz Burj might just be the oldest traffic circle in the world; but in a city strewn with ruins, it hardly receives a second glance. Cars careen and whiz past the monument at its center as they navigate the tar road that snakes around it at the busy intersection, which connects the Lodhi Road and Mathura Road.

Very little is known about the structure, except that it may have been built in the 1500s or perhaps even a century earlier, preceding the buildings at Humayun's tombs, making it an early Mughal-era monument. The intricate green, blue, and yellow tilework on the octagonal façade suggests that it was built for someone important; but there is no record of who lies in the unique tomb it shelters, or who it was commissioned by. Originally named Subz Burj, meaning the "green dome," it is now called the Neeli Chattri, or the "blue umbrella," reportedly due to a restoration snafu that occurred while the monument was being spruced up for the Commonwealth Games in 2010: the dome was mistakenly retiled blue instead of green.

For an uncomplicated roundabout, it carries a great legacy: representing the architectural influences that came from Central Asia. Resembling Istanbul's blue dome rather than following the Indo-Islamic style that Mughal structures in India are associated with, it is one of the few examples of a double dome balanced on a high drum in Delhi. It is often confused with the nearby blue-domed Neela Gumbad, which is not as distinctively styled.

Oddly, the Subz Burj once served as a British police station; and the image of an Englishman sitting within the high-recessed dome surrounded by dainty Persian artwork is quite an entertaining thought. For now, it has accepted its newly acquired hue and its role as perhaps the world's oldest roundabout, as it stands quietly glinting in the sun, overlooking the constant buzz of traffic.

Address Intersection of Lodhi and Mathura Roads, Nizamuddin | **Getting there** JLN Stadium Metro Station (Violet Line); Pragati Maidan Metro Station (Blue Line) | **Hours** All day. Entry inside the tomb is restricted. | **Tip** Humayun's Tomb is one of Delhi's most visited monuments, and for good reason. It is the birthplace of the Indo-Islamic style of architecture and is said to be the inspiration for the Taj Mahal.

99 Sufi Inayat Khan Music Academy

The universal mystic's song

Just when you think you have uncovered all of Nizamuddin Basti's mysteries, the neighbourhood reveals another delightful secret. A stroll down Hazrat Nizamuddin's *dargah* (shrine) complex, through a maze of narrow lanes, uneven stairways, and low arches, leads to a pristine white compound. The wings of a kite holding aloft a heart, a symbol of Sufism, adorn the walls, marking the *dargah* of the Hazrat Inayat Khan (1882–1927).

Hazrat Inayat Khan, an accomplished musician, was conferred the title of Tansen (master of melody) by the Nizam of Hyderabad. He had started touring in the West, and was encouraged by his teacher to spread the Sufi message of love through music. Hazrat Inayat Khan's teachings are widespread and his followers come from all over the world to visit the *dargah* during his *Urs* (death anniversary of a Sufi saint).

The lower level of the *dargah* serves as the Sufi Inayat Khan Music Academy. The belief that one can attain divine grace through the arts is nourished at this school. It offers courses in Hindustani classical music, poetry, *qawwali*, and calligraphy. The peaceful villa-like interior with lattice screens and clean Zen-like lines nurtures creativity. The lush courtyard serves as a serene refuge in which a *shagird* (music student) may practice. The tomes in the library provide an opportunity to delve deeper into the history of Sufism.

On Friday evenings, musical greats like Ustad Meraj Ahmed Nizami and Chand Nizami perform their compositions at the shrine on the upper level. The tomb of Hazrat Inayat Khan shares space with a tree, and the shrine is built around it, enveloping nature within its fold. This is a more restrained sanctuary of Sufi faith – a place that resonates with the message of oneness, of all paths leading to the same destination.

Address 129 Basti Nizamuddin, Nizamuddin, www.dargahsufi-inayat.org, info@dargahsufi-inayat.org, Tel +91 11 24350833 | **Getting there** Jangpura Metro Station (Violet Line) | **Hours** Sat–Thu 10am–5pm, Fri 6pm onwards | **Tip** You can check the cultural programs and the social initiatives undertaken by the *dargah* on their website. Music, poetry, and calligraphy courses are on offer here for Indian and international students.

درگاہ شریف
حضرت صوفی عنایت خان

दरगाह शरीफ़
हज़रत सूफ़ी इनायत ख़ान

...AT INAYAT KHAN MEMORIAL TRUS...

DARGAH

...NAYAT KHAN

100__ Sujan Singh Park
Delhi's most exclusive address

Don't let the name Sujan Singh Park confuse you. It is not exactly a park, but a residential block near the popular Khan Market. Built around a small courtyard, this square of 84 flats, with its arched entrance and colonial-style apartments with high ceilings, fireplaces, and grand bathrooms is low profile despite its market value. One of the most exclusive addresses in Delhi, it is the former home of builder Sobha Singh (1890–1978), known more famously as the man who laid the foundation stones of New Delhi. The story of Sujan Singh Park is therefore the story of New Delhi too.

In the book *Celebrating Delhi,* the life of Sobha Singh and his contribution to the city was beautifully recounted by his son, the prolific Indian author and famous journalist Khushwant Singh (1915–2014). As an 18-year-old contractor, Sobha Singh moved the foundation stones from Kingsway Camp to the new proposed site in Raisina Hill. This was done under the cover of darkness, so as to ward off bad omens. The stones were carried in a bullock cart with only the light of a Petromax lamp. Sobha Singh rode alongside on a bicycle. He became one of the contractors who made Edward Lutyens' and Herbert Baker's dream of building an exemplary capital city that instilled faith and order in the Indian masses a reality. The India Gate and the Jaipur column are the most notable among the many buildings constructed by Sobha Singh. He named everything after his father, hence the name Sujan Singh crops up all over the city.

The red brick building from 1945 is now mostly occupied by Sobha Singh's descendants. It once served as barracks for English soldiers during the Second World War. Privy to many elite soirees, the address is also popular as the former home of Khushwant Singh. The message, "Don't ring this bell unless you are expected" can be still found on his door.

Address Sujan Singh Park, Subramania Bharti Marg | Getting there Khan Market Metro Station (Violet Line) | Hours As it's a private residence, Sujan Singh Park is inaccessible to visitors, but the guards might allow you in the courtyard for a quick look if you ask nicely. | Tip Spend a pleasant afternoon at Khan Market, a high-end market with eclectic book shops, quaint cafes, and artisanal boutiques.

101 Sultan Garhi's Mausoleum

The country's first Islamic tomb

An old, craggy-faced man wearing a red chequered scarf sits at the marble entrance of the Sultan Garhi complex, reading a small prayer book, turning his beads. The historical significance of the country's oldest existing mausoleum, though, is easily lost in the bustling, modern suburb of Vasant Kunj, with its malls and burgeoning construction sites.

The fort-like tomb was built between 1200 and 1236, during the short-lived reign of Prince Nasir-ud-din Mahmud, the second son of Sultan Iltutmish. The prince was killed on the battlefield, leaving behind an aggrieved father who had once conferred upon his son the title of *Malik-Us-Sharq*, or Nasir-ud-din, meaning the "King of the East." Saddened by his death, Iltutmish built the octagonal tomb, which is believed incomplete – lacking the traditional *chhatri* (cupola) common to other Mughal tombs – since Iltutmish himself died a few short years later.

Visited by few tourists today, this structure is of great spiritual significance to local Hindus as well as Muslims, who light incense and pray here every Thursday. They climb down the winding stone stairway to the chamber beneath the tomb and ply the royal saint with offerings of ghee, milk, roasted gram, jiggery, and rose petals.

Within the complex, there are also the remnants of a Tuqlaq-era well and a mosque. Particularly splendid is the delicately engraved *mihrab* (wall that indicates the direction of Mecca), repaired by Feroz Shah Tuqlaq, which stands in contrast to the grayish-red stone setting. In the midst of screeching parrots and airplane spotting, Sultan Garhi provides an interesting peek into the beginning of an Indo-Islamic architectural style as well as the complexity of faith and its interplay with modernity.

Address Near Sector C, Pocket 9, Vasant Kunj, Malakpur Kohli Village | Getting there Chattarpur Metro Station (Yellow Line) | Hours Daily, sunrise to sunset. Entrance fee: Rs 100 for foreign tourists | Tip Hang out at Monkey Bar (Plot 11, upper ground floor, LSC, Pocket C 6 & 7, Vasant Kunj), the local pub, and play a game of pool or foosball.

102_ Sunder Nursery

The birthplace of Delhi's tree-lined avenues

A heady combination of roses mixed with freshly cut grass and a hint of wet earth greets a chance visitor to this perfumed cradle of nature close to the Humayun's Tomb complex. Spread across 70 acres, Azim Bagh (as it was earlier known) is India's largest government nursery. In 1929, while envisaging Delhi's eighth city, British urban planners used this sanctuary as a laboratory to experiment with and select trees that would serve as sentries for Delhi's majestic avenues. Saplings from all over India and British colonies around the world were evaluated to arrive at the perfect specimens worthy of Imperial India's new capital. As a result, rare and unusual tree species like the Pink Cedar, Atalantia, Khasi, and West Indian Elm are found within the boundaries of this ecological treasure box.

The idyllic surroundings of the nursery attract very few visitors. The pathways – some neglected, some restored – lead you on a journey through the grand visions of the Mughal era. The *charbagh*, a preferred garden style, complements the splendour of the 500-year-old Sunderwala Burj and Lakkar Burj. Sights of lone visitors napping in the Mughal pavilion aren't uncommon, while squirrels scamper across Sunderwala Mahal, butterflies busy themselves at the arboretum, and birds survey the Grand Trunk Road of yore.

Restoration is under way at a furious pace, with masons and nursery workers trying to meet deadlines set by various authorities to open a world-class urban park at Sunder Nursery. In another corner, environmentalists and experts toil to create four microhabitats to house a mini-cosmos of Delhi's native ecosystems – *Dabar* (Marshy), *Kohi* (Hill), *Khadar* (Riverine), and *Bangar* (Alluvial). In the midst of all this activity, zealous gardeners haggle over the prices of prized rose, poppy, and herb plants. What once was a Mughal gardener's vision of paradise is today an urban gardener's dream come true.

Address National Zoological Park, Sundar Nagar, Nizamuddin | Getting there Jangpura Metro Station (Blue Line) | Hours Mon – Sat 9am – 4pm | Tip There is no better nursery to pick up a few plants. It's where Delhi's greenest thumbs come to dress their home gardens with rare plants of great pedigree.

103 Swantantra Senani Smarak

The country's most haunted place

Tucked away in a far corner of the Red Fort complex in Delhi, the Salimgarh Fort (now rechristened) is deserted even though thousands of visitors swarm the Red Fort daily. One reason could be that the Salimgarh Fort has a reputation that precedes it: as a haunted house of horrors. Even Salim Shah, son of Sher Shah Suri, who built the structure in 1546 on an island on the Yamuna River, couldn't have foreseen the grim events that would taint his fort-palace. Only the building's skeleton remains, with a long walk over a masonry bridge connecting it to the Red Fort.

Built by Shah Jahan in 1638, the Red Fort is the only Mughal structure with an asymmetrical boundary, which allowed the newer fort to absorb the old fort and its bastions into its ramparts. Salimgarh Fort soon evolved into the "pet dungeon" of Delhi's rulers. From Salim Shah to Humayun, Shah Jahan to the British – all kept the dungeon keepers busy by meting out torture and death sentences to dissenters brought to this place.

The Freedom Fighters' Memorial, established in the British barracks where soldiers were imprisoned, is an attempt to add some context to the depressing cells. In the eerie silences between the rumblings of trains passing nearby, browse through Indian National Army uniforms, personal belongings of soldiers, and an array of sepia-tinted photographs.

Stories of hauntings permeate the impenetrable walls. Aurangzeb's daughter Zebunissa, who was incarcerated here by her father, is said to travel the corridors and float up the stairs singing her poems. There is a sense of being followed, perhaps intensified by the gaze of army personnel stationed here. Whispers and footsteps seem to echo in the walls of the jail, as if saying, "I dare you …"

Address Red Fort, Netaji Subhash Marg, Chandni Chowk | Getting there Chandni Chowk Metro Station (Yellow Line) | Hours Tue–Sun 10am–4pm | Tip At the Mumtaz Mahal (Red Fort), the personal effects of the former royal inhabitants, like ink pots, daggers, carpets, cushions, lithographs, arms, and other things, are displayed in six galleries.

104_Tihar Food Court

A restaurant run by prison inmates

Visiting a prison, even if it is Tihar, the largest prison complex in South Asia, is highly unusual unless you know someone incarcerated there. Yet, the Tihar Jail is now on the public's dining map, courtesy of the prison's new restaurant (started in July 2014). This jail is no stranger to innovative programs, and the restaurant is a part of its novel approach of giving inmates a shot at dignity and purpose in life after their release.

The Tihar Food Court looks like a normal restaurant with outdoor and indoor dining areas. A stern constable oversees the inmates working here, who have been chosen for their good behaviour. Part of their reward is being allowed to cycle or walk to work via an external road even though there's a way through the jail.

Within the unexpectedly calm, quiet environs, an unusual tradition has gathered steam. Many who visit this restaurant are driven by the belief that consuming food made by prisoners living a hard life is a way of alleviating bad luck. In fact, astrologers advise this method of eliminating a *dosha* (fault in horoscope) to their patrons. This bodes well for the restaurant as it generates traffic, which has helped it become self-sustaining.

The menu is uncomplicated, with regular Indian fare like *samosas*, *kachoris*, sandwiches, *dosas*, and *roti-sabzi*. The restaurant even offers a home delivery service. In fact, there is nothing that distinguishes Tihar from a normal restaurant, except that you are sitting just feet away from a prison and being served by convicted inmates trained at a premier hospitality school.

Graffiti and a poignant Hindi poem in bold type running along the length of the prison boundary verbalise the management's resolve to strengthen the use of the prison as a correctional facility where individuals get a second chance. Surely, you will not find a bite of food more meaningful anywhere else in the world.

Address Tihar Jail Complex (opposite Indraprastha Gas Station), Jail Road,
Tel +91 11 28525639 | **Getting there** Tilak Nagar Metro Station (Blue Line) | **Hours**
Mon–Sat 11am–3pm & 5pm–9pm | **Tip** The shop Tihar Haat is also run by inmates,
and has quality food, furniture, handicrafts, and woven products made by the prisoners.

105 __ The Treat
A Rajesh Khanna fan's dedication

Only a few know of this small food kiosk in the neighbourhood of embassies in the diplomatic and upscale enclave of Chanakyapuri. More than the food served here, it's the story of how the Treat came to be that draws its regulars back. The famous actor-turned-politician Rajesh Khanna (1942 – 2012) gifted the place to the owner in 1994, and urged him to start a catering and restaurant business. And the only reason this devoted fan did so, with no training in cooking, was because his demi-god asked him to.

The owner, 60-year-old Vipin Oberoi, is a diehard fan of Khanna, known as the first superstar of the Hindi film industry (and later a member of Parliament). His friendship with the late actor is immortalised in this little food cart. It is plastered with images of Khanna from both his on-screen and off-screen life. In a country where temples are erected in the names of Bollywood celebrities, this is instead a place where a movie star honoured a fan, by being a good friend.

The soundtrack of the film *Anand*, in which Khanna portrays a terminally ill patient bringing joy to the lives he touches, plays in the background. The mood is set for an evening of mutton *korma*, *chaap*, honey-chilli potato chips, and kebabs. Listening to Vipin talk about his memories of his idol is a delight. Their camaraderie is evident in the sepia images of a young Rajesh Khanna and Vipin Oberoi taken during election campaigns. Introduced by a relative, Oberoi confesses that his only ambition was to be a friend of the superstar, and as you watch him taking food orders and managing the restaurant, you know that it is still the same feeling that drives him.

Twice a year (on the birthday and the death anniversary of Rajesh Khanna), Vipin forgoes his business interests and treats friends, family, and customers to free dinners and a huge celebration.

Address Sun Chick Caterers (behind Jesus & Mary College), Rizal Marg, Chanakyapuri, Tel +91 9999780101 | **Getting there** Race Course Metro Station (Yellow Line) | **Hours** Mon–Sun 2.30pm–12.30am | **Tip** The Nehru Park (Vinay Marg, Ramnagar, Chanakyapuri), a popular picnic spot a few minutes away, is a great venue for music, food, and art events. A large statue of Lenin stands in the park, a testimony to the once deep political bonds between India and Russia.

106__ Triveni Terrace Café

An intellectual's haunt

It is perhaps the appeal of walking barefoot in the small open-air auditorium of the Triveni Kala Sangam that makes it a favourite haunt of artists, writers, and radicals; or maybe it's the tiny cafe that has long been a part of the thriving Arts and Crafts Centre, housing the Department of Art, Dance, and Music. The cafe's plastic seating and *garam chai* (hot tea) that once found favour with artists M. F. Hussain and Vasudeo S. Gaitonde have given way to white wrought-iron chairs, ceramic planters, and tiny pickle *barnis* (porcelain jars) used as condiment containers. Though slightly fancier today, the heart of Triveni Terrace is still the same.

A cat sits lazily on the parapet near the awning, enjoying the filtered light of Joseph Stein's iconic 1950s structure. On the opposite terrace, a photography class is in progress. People amble into the exhibition spaces while the artists chat with art aficionados and gallery administrators, sipping tea in the outdoor auditorium.

Triveni Kala Sangam was erected during a time of greater artistic freedom, when the idea of building a new India was emerging. The construction of a new country also gave lease to a new artistic freedom, and Triveni Kala Sangam was a big part of it. Even today, the small canteen continues to fiercely protect its ethos of nurturing artists' souls.

The regular favourites, like *keema* (minced meat), *shami* kebabs, and *pakoras* (fried dumplings) have seen entire generations of broke college students and artists through lean periods. The redesign means that the cafe, to the delight of *Dilliwallahs*, is one of the few places that serve *poha*, a West Indian dish. Indoors, a few business types at a community table type furiously while an elderly art browser flicks through a newspaper. The Triveni Terrace remains a hidden gem that nourishes creative minds amidst a peaceful and inspiring setting.

Address Triveni Kala Sangam, 205 Tansen Marg | **Getting there** Mandi House Metro Station (Blue/Violet Line) | **Hours** Mon–Sat 10.30am–3.30pm & 4.30 pm–6.30pm | **Tip** The National Museum of Natural History just around the corner will stun you right at the lobby with an enormous life-sized stuffed rhinoceros. The tea seller outside serves the best chai in Delhi in *kulhads* (clay tumblers).

107 __ Urdu Bazaar
The katibs of Urdu market

Despite being a small stretch of shops, the Urdu Bazaar is an intrinsic part of Old Delhi. When the British destroyed the original market as a consequence of the 1857 Uprising, Ghalib said, "When Urdu Bazar is no more, where is Urdu? By God, Delhi is no more a city, but a camp, a cantonment. No fort, no city, no bazaar."

When he penned this, Ghalib was certainly thinking of the bazaar's inherent grace. The cultured bookshops hosted the city's literati, who would browse for titles written in the familiar tongue of their homelands. It's changed now. The meaty smoke of kebabs swirls through the market, dominating the musty smell of books. Still, it is one of the few places where the lyrical words of Urdu still hang in the air. Little shops with names like Rashid & Sons, Maktaba Jama Limited, and Kutub Khana Anjuman-e-Taraqqi-e Urdu bravely square their shoulders against the spreading tea shops armed with vats of oil sizzling with *samosas* and *jalebi* (snacks).

There aren't too many bookshops left here. Those few that remain are the custodians of books published in Urdu – rare Persian manuscripts, humble journals, and texts. Outside the shops you sometimes find a *katib*, a traditional calligrapher. Calligraphy panels etched in marble and stone, and dressed with jewels, are an indelible part of Delhi's monuments. But the *katibs* will soon leave too. Calligraphers are called upon on fewer occasions these days. Now the script only appears on marriage announcements, yearly calendars, certificates, election pamphlets, and invitations for *iftaar* (gatherings to end a fast) during the odd month of Ramzan.

There are even computers that now imitate the hand of a calligrapher, but the magic of uneven lines and ink blots that linger when a nib pauses is a beautiful sight. For a demonstration of this ancient art in its original setting, visit the Urdu Bazaar before it's too late.

Address Urdu Bazaar, Jama Masjid | Getting there Chawri Bazaar Metro Station (Yellow Line) | Hours Mon–Fri 10am–6pm | Tip The restaurant Karim's (Jama Masjid, Gate 2) is a foodie's mecca, visited by meat lovers for its delectable *nihari* (bone-marrow stew), kebabs, mutton korma, and biryani.

108__Urdu Park
The Delhi Wrestling Federation hangout

Parks in Delhi usually have distinct personalities. Rajpath Gardens are stately, Lodhi Park is demure, and Nehru Park is renowned for its scenic beauty. The tiny Urdu Park can be pegged as one that is bursting with character. Its place in history is secure as the spot where leaders like Maulana Azad whipped up support for the fight against the British Raj. And though it does have trees, plants, lawns, and all the other usual trappings of a park, it isn't exactly a tranquil paradise.

Mostly, tired cycle-rickshaw wallahs, labourers, and workers in the Old City rest in Urdu's shaded areas. The cheers from an ongoing cricket match act as the perfect white noise. However, the casual atmosphere suddenly buzzes with excitement and energy on just one day, every week. On Sundays, the park fills up with anticipation as it hosts the hugely popular sport of *kushti* (wrestling). The various *akharas* (wrestling schools) gather to have bouts at the Urdu Park *dangal* (wrestling competition). There's cheering and hooting, and everyone has their favourites. Little boys wrestle fiercely while young men compete with more restraint and finesse. Even though the onlookers hogging the benches and spreading out on the grass around the sand pitch are not aware of it, they are part of a local tradition. Urdu Park is a kind of old boys' club of Old Delhi.

The masseurs of Urdu Park have a formidable reputation of offering the best open-air *champi* (head massages) in Delhi. They slather oil and knead and twist the muscles until a customer is free from knots and aches. The ear cleaners spread their tools on a piece of cloth as carefully as a surgeon, selecting the right pointy implement for brave souls. Young boys hang around, fiddling with their mobiles or just people-watching. Outside the park, street vendors peddle their wares with energy and attitude.

Address Near Meena Bazaar, Daryanganj, Chandni Chowk | Getting there Chawri Bazaar Metro Station (Yellow Line) | Hours Park: daily, sunrise to sunset. Wrestling matches: Sun 4pm onwards | Tip Right next door to the small park is the Netaji Subhash Chandra Park, dedicated to freedom fighter Subhash Chandra Bose.

109_ Yadgar-e-Zauq
The rescued tomb of the king of poets

In the shadowy alleyways of Multani Dhanda in Paharganj, you'll find the tomb of Sheikh Muhammad Ibrahim Zauq, the court poet of Emperor Bahadur Shah Zafar. The placement of his tomb fulfils his expressed wish: "Who could bear to leave the beloved alleys of Delhi?" he once wrote.

A few years ago, Yadgar-e-Zauq was lost to the indignity of public toilets built over his tomb. Vigilantes campaigned and petitioned until the Supreme Court ordered a committee to verify the exact location of the grave. The toilets were torn down, and the grave was rebuilt over a 750-square-meter piece of land. The comedy of errors (now corrected) continued with a plaque in English calling Zauq the Parrot of India, as a mistranslation of his title *Khaqan-i-hind* (Nightingale of India).

Son of a poor soldier, Zauq became the toast of *mushairas* (poetry recitals). Soon, Meer Kazim Husain Beqarar, the court poet, took notice of the young Zauq. He shaped Zauq's clean, controlled verse, and his career. Zauq eventually became mentor to the emperor, Shah Zafar. His rivalry with his contemporary, Ghalib, another great poet of the time, was legendary. Ghalib's wit and flair had many admirers, but Zauq, with his severe style, was considered superior. Their stinging couplets taunting each other entertain and amuse even today.

To reach Zauq's tomb you'll have to navigate a bustling market, then weave through winding nameless alleyways. Plants and creepers adorn the warm terra-cotta-coloured walls of the plain memorial. A sandstone plinth, crowned by a marble tomb and a few marble plaques, marks the grave of the poet.

The lit *shama* (lamp) of Delhi's *mehfils* (gatherings) seems distant here. But Zauq's poignant poetry has found a modern admirer in the form of Hindi cinema. His verses continue to be immortalised in Bollywood songs.

यादगारे ज़ौक़

YADGAR-E-ZAUQ

Address Gali No. 6 (near Punjab National Bank, DB Gupta Road), Paharganj, nearest landmark is Dargah Qadam Sharif | **Getting there** Ramakrishna Ashram Marg Metro Station (Blue Line) | **Hours** Daily, sunrise to sunset | **Tip** Sitaram Diwan Chand Bhature Wala (2243, Rajguru Marg, Chuna Mandi, Paharganj) is an extremely popular eatery that is considered the best place in Delhi to savour a dish called *chole bhature* (chickpeas and fried bread).

110_ Yamuna Biodiversity Park

A man-made miracle of nature

A setting straight out of Rudyard Kipling's *The Jungle Book* awaits you at the Yamuna Biodiversity Park. The hard work of environmental scientists from Delhi University has transformed a barren land into a 453-acre repository of vanishing flora and fauna, right in the heart of the city. This verdant enclave consists of Phase I, the restricted section, where guided tours can be arranged on request; and Phase II, which is open to visitors.

As a result of the influences of the Mughals, the British, and now the rapid urbanisation of modern India, the city's original natural heritage has been dwindling over the past 100 years. Yet here, spread before you, is an almost extinct ecology that once flourished all along the Yamuna River.

The wetlands and two simulated natural water bodies are the park's most attractive features and are home to hundreds of migratory birds from Central Asia, Siberia, and Europe. Birders and wildlife photographers arrive at the park with ambitions of spotting red-crested pochards. Around you, scaly-breasted munia hover over Buddha-belly and golden bamboo. The butterfly conservatory is filled with the gleeful calls of young visitors who haven't seen butterflies in a very long time. Hares bound about without fear in the sacred grove. As you walk among the protected, local fruit-bearing trees grown here, like khirni, sapota, jamun, amla (Indian gooseberry), lemon, orange, grape, loquat, and ber, you understand the true magnitude of the loss suffered by Delhi's native flora, wiped out by invasive species like the *vilayati kikar* (mesquite tree).

The recreated environment contains ten mounds that display miniature forest ecosystems.

A guided tour is the most informative way of venturing into the semi-wild area, and the Nature Interpretation Centre is a good place to learn more about the jungle out there.

Address Milan Vihar, Wazirabad | **Getting there** GTB Nagar Metro Station (Yellow Line) | **Hours** Mon–Fri 9.30am–6pm; guided tours 10am–4pm (book in advance) | **Tip** On your way back, stop at Majnu ka Tilla, a Tibetan refugee colony that has become a hub for great food and handmade woollies, just right for Delhi winters. A bowl of *thukpa* or a plate of *momos* at Tee Dee's (32, Aruna Nagar, Majnu ka Tila) with some ginger-honey tea is highly recommended.

111_Yogmaya Temple

The only surviving pre-Sultanate temple

It's easy to miss this temple concealed among the houses at Lal Kot on the main Qutb Road to Mehrauli village. According to folklore, the original temple was built by the Pandavas (the five brothers in the Hindu epic *Mahabharata*) to honour Lord Krishna's sister Yogmaya. Yogmaya, a form of the Goddess Durga, was the baby who King Kamsa slayed after it was prophesied that the eighth child – Krishna – born to his sister Devaki was destined to kill him. Instructed by Lord Vishnu, King Vasudeva (Krishna's father) smuggled his son out of prison and put Yogmaya in his place. Before disappearing in a flash of light, Yogmaya told Kamsa that Krishna was still alive and would kill him.

A dazzling five-hooded mirrored snake head greets you at the entrance. But that's where the sparkle ends. In a city of bold, striking temples, the soothing marble interior and simplicity of Yogmaya is refreshing. The display featuring the eight forms of Vishnu is the pièce de résistance. The colourful *pankhas* (hand-operated fans) inside the temple are part of *Phool Walon ki Sair* (the festival of flower sellers). Yogmaya serves as a pit stop for this annual fête, which dates back to 1812. The story goes that when Queen Mumtaz's son mistakenly fired on Sir Archibald Seton, the British Resident, she vowed to organise a procession to honour all the deities if he was pardoned. He was released, and the procession was established by the Mughal emperor Akbar Shah II, to fulfil the queen's promise.

Even after the monsoons, the procession, carrying flower *chadors* (coverings), *pankhas*, and offerings, makes its way from Chandni Chowk to the Yogmaya Temple, continuing to the shrine of Qutbuddin Bakhtiar Kaki before culminating at the *jharna* (stream) at Hauz-i-Shamsi. The three-day event is an exemplary display of harmony between Hindus and Muslims, and is possibly the best time to visit the temple.

Address Khasra No. 1806, Mehrauli | **Getting there** Qutb Minar Metro Station (Yellow Line) | **Hours** Daily 6am–8pm | **Tip** The Olive Bar & Kitchen (One Style Mile, Haveli 6, Kalka Das Marg, Mehrauli, noon–3pm & 7.30pm–midnight) offers a beautiful dining experience. Reserve a table under the giant banyan tree and enjoy a Mediterranean meal beneath the stars for a romantic evening.

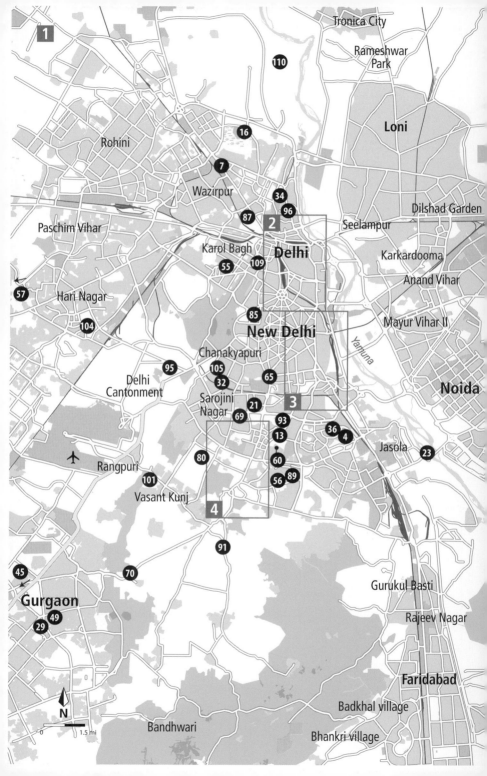

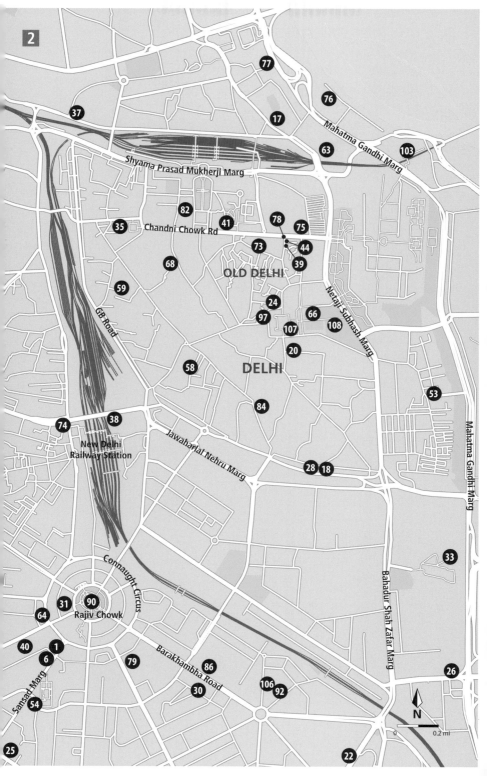

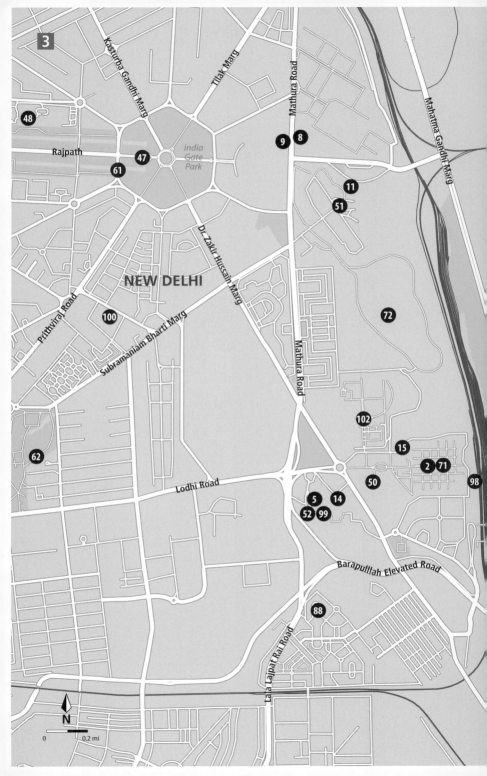

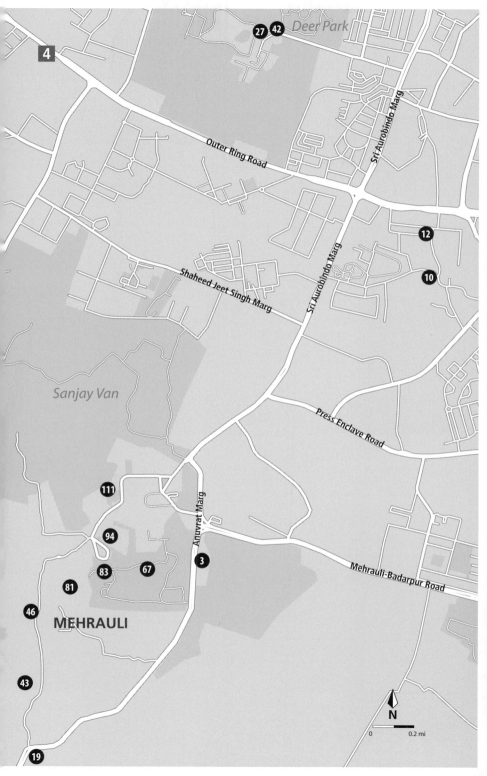

Lucia Jay von Seldeneck,
Carolin Huder, Verena Eidel
**111 PLACES IN BERLIN
THAT YOU SHOULDN'T MISS**
ISBN 978-3-95451-208-9

Rüdiger Liedtke
**111 PLACES IN MUNICH
THAT YOU SHOULDN'T MISS**
ISBN 978-3-95451-222-5

Frank McNally
**111 PLACES IN DUBLIN
THAT YOU SHOULDN'T MISS**
ISBN 978-3-95451-649-0

Rike Wolf
**111 PLACES IN HAMBURG
THAT YOU SHOULDN'T MISS**
ISBN 978-3-95451-234-8

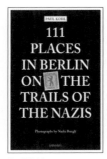

Paul Kohl
**111 PLACES IN BERLIN
ON THE TRAIL OF THE NAZIS**
ISBN 978-3-95451-323-9

Peter Eickhoff
**111 PLACES IN VIENNA
THAT YOU SHOULDN'T MISS**
ISBN 978-3-95451-206-5

Sharon Fernandes
**111 PLACES IN NEW DELHI
THAT YOU MUST NOT MISS**
ISBN 978-3-95451-648-3

Sally Asher, Michael Murphy
**111 PLACES IN NEW ORLEANS
THAT YOU MUST NOT MISS**
ISBN 978-3-95451-645-2

Gordon Streisand
**111 PLACES IN MIAMI
AND THE KEYS
THAT YOU MUST NOT MISS**
ISBN 978-3-95451-644-5

Dirk Engelhardt
111 PLACES IN BARCELONA
THAT YOU MUST NOT MISS
ISBN 978-3-95451-353-6

Rüdiger Liedtke
111 PLACES ON MALLORCA
THAT YOU SHOULDN'T MISS
ISBN 978-3-95451-281-2

Marcus X. Schmid
111 PLACES IN ISTANBUL
THAT YOU MUST NOT MISS
ISBN 978-3-95451-423-6

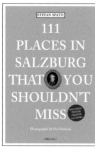

Stefan Spath
111 PLACES IN SALZBURG
THAT YOU SHOULDN'T MISS
ISBN 978-3-95451-230-0

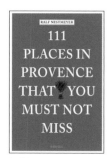

Ralf Nestmeyer
111 PLACES IN PROVENCE
THAT YOU MUST NOT MISS
ISBN 978-3-95451-422-9

Christiane Bröcker,
Babette Schröder
111 PLACES IN STOCKHOLM
THAT YOU MUST NOT MISS
ISBN 978-3-95451-459-5

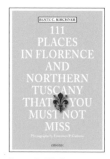

Beate C. Kirchner
111 PLACES IN FLORENCE
AND NORTHERN TUSCANY
THAT YOU MUST NOT MISS
ISBN 978-3-95451-613-1

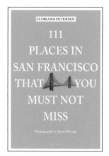

Floriana Petersen, Steve Werney
111 PLACES IN SAN FRANCISCO
THAT YOU MUST NOT MISS
ISBN 978-3-95451-609-4

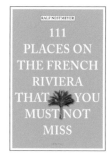

Ralf Nestmeyer
111 PLACES ON THE
FRENCH RIVIERA
THAT YOU MUST NOT MISS
ISBN 978-3-95451-612-4

Gerd Wolfgang Sievers
**111 PLACES IN VENICE
THAT YOU MUST NOT MISS**
ISBN 978-3-95451-460-1

Petra Sophia Zimmermann
**111 PLACES IN VERONA
AND LAKE GARDA THAT
YOU MUST NOT MISS**
ISBN 978-3-95451-611-7

Rüdiger Liedtke,
Laszlo Trankovits
**111 PLACES IN CAPE TOWN
THAT YOU MUST NOT MISS**
ISBN 978-3-95451-610-0

Gillian Tait
**111 PLACES IN EDINBURGH
THAT YOU SHOULDN'T MISS**
ISBN 978-3-95451-883-8

Laurel Moglen, Julia Posey
**111 PLACES IN LOS ANGELES
THAT YOU SHOULDN'T MISS**
ISBN 978-3-95451-884-5

Giulia Castelli Gattinara,
Mario Verin
**111 PLACES IN MILAN
THAT YOU MUST NOT MISS**
ISBN 978-3-95451-331-4

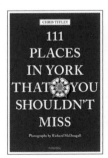

John Sykes
**111 PLACES IN LONDON
THAT YOU SHOULDN'T MISS**
ISBN 978-3-95451-346-8

Julian Treuherz,
Peter de Figueiredo
**111 PLACES IN LIVERPOOL
THAT YOU SHOULDN'T MISS**
ISBN 978-3-95451-769-5

Chris Titley
**111 PLACES IN YORK
THAT YOU SHOULDN'T MISS**
ISBN 978-3-95451-768-8

Annett Klingner
**111 PLACES IN ROME
THAT YOU MUST NOT MISS**
ISBN 978-3-95451-469-4

Jo-Anne Elikann
**111 PLACES IN NEW YORK
THAT YOU MUST NOT MISS**
ISBN 978-3-95451-052-8

Kirstin von Glasow
**111 COFFEESHOPS IN
LONDON THAT YOU MUST
NOT MISS**
ISBN 978-3-95451-614-8

Mark Gabor, Susan Lusk
**111 SHOPS IN NEW YORK
THAT YOU MUST NOT MISS**
ISBN 978-3-95451-351-2

Kirstin von Glasow
**111 SHOPS IN LONDON
THAT YOU SHOULDN'T MISS**
ISBN 978-3-95451-341-3

Desa Philadelphia
**111 SHOPS IN LOS ANGELES
THAT YOU MUST NOT MISS**
ISBN 978-3-95451-615-5

Aylie Lonmon
**111 SHOPS IN MILAN
THAT YOU MUST NOT MISS**
ISBN 978-3-95451-637-7

Acknowledgements

For Tushar A. Amin – part mentor, critic, sounding board, and supporter – who has been a part of my journey from the first to the last page.

I am grateful for the invaluable leads and the help extended by friends and friends-of-friends while writing the book: Jivitha Crasta, Maria Mathai, Himanshu Verma (Red Earth), Yuveka Singh (Darwesh), Ameet Singh, Shashank Samant, Annie Zaidi, Monica Bathija, Maneka Agarwal, and Ashish Gupta.

Also, a big thank you to the strangers who pointed me to the right places, the guards who let me through locked doors, and the warmth of the people who revealed personal experiences based on their favourite spaces in Delhi.

—S.F.

The Author

Sharon Fernandes is a writer/editor who has worked with various publications, including *ELLE India* and *BBC Travel*. Devoted to the curation of experiences and stories, she has written on travel, literature, culture, art, fashion, and feminism. She experiments with content that creates a bridge between old-school journalism and new-media tools. Sharon lists her big travel adventure as the time she took a year off to explore the country with just a backpack. When not writing, she loves exploring traditional bazaars and old city areas for inspiration.

The Photographer

Growing up in a defence services family, **Tarunima Sen**'s early life was filled with constant travel and the exploration of new places. Experiencing these many different cultures, from Botswana (Africa) to West Bengal (India), has shaped who she is today. Among her professional credits, she is the co-author of *Bhopal Survivors Speak*, a book based on her experience living with and learning about the survivors of the Bhopal Gas Tragedy. Tarunima is currently a freelance photographer based out of New Delhi.